ALAN KONELL

Partnership
Tools

Published in US by
Hippo Press
P.O. Box 12948
Raleigh, NC 27605 U.S.A.

Design by Suzanne Eismann
Manufactured in the United States of America

Cataloging in Publication Data
Konell, Alan
Partnership Tools: Transforming the Way We Live Together
1. Marriage
2. Communication in Marriage
3. Interpersonal Relations
4. Intimacy (Psychology)
HQ734
646.78
Library of Congress Catalog Card number: 97-67259
ISBN 0-9702992-0-6

To my mother Claire,
my wife Barbara, and
my daughters Marissa
and Mallory.

Tools

Acknowledgments

I would like to thank all of you who have helped me and supported me in writing this book. Some helped more directly than others did, but all of you were essential to me.

I would like to thank Reid Wilson, Peter Guzzardi, Suzanne Eismann, Renee Prillaman, Deb Eaker, Reid Boates, Doug Mann, Rodney Buchner, Tarn-Taran Singh, Richard Bergman, David Harold, Marty Solomon, Howard Konell, Virginia Cassell, Jane Dyer, Paul Oakes, Eileen Beechinor, Mary Votta, Tina Gibson and Roxie Hayes.

I especially want to acknowledge the four women who in my life have taught me the most about relationships: my daughters, Marissa and Mallory, my mother, Claire, and most of all, my wonderful wife, Barbara.

Preface

This book has been a long time coming. For years I've been writing down all my profound and not so profound insights about relationships and being human. In my twenties I was impressed with how much I knew. Now, almost fifty, I'm impressed with how much I don't know. I am very excited about what I will be learning in my future and hope that what I have shared with you in this book will help with your learning.

I decided to write a book on relationships when I was sitting in my office one day, about ten years ago, after saying something that seemed to significantly affect the couple sitting in front of me. They commented that how I framed what was going on in their relationship made them feel more optimistic about their ability to make their relationship work. I realized that what I had said could as easily have been shared with a dozen or even hundreds of couples that might have benefitted from what I offered to them. Having always had the desire to make as big a contribution as I could, I realized that seeing one couple at a time might not be my most efficient format. It was then that I decided to write a book.

I'm glad that I'm a late bloomer. This is my first book. But if I had written one earlier, it would not be what I think this one is. I am thankful for all of the people who have allowed me to practice on them while helping me to support my family while I learned.

I have been fortunate to have many wonderful teachers who taught me how to look for the structure and patterns of human interaction. I seem to have the ability to create simple, but effective models that many people have used to successfully transform their relationships. This book is my attempt to share some of these understandings with you who can then use your intelligence and desire to have healthy relationships to create a better life for yourself and all those whom you love and care about. You may even find that the ideas offered in this book will empower you to be able to care about more people in a healthy way.

I am always humbled by the resilience that human beings demonstrate. So many times I have witnessed people recover from dire experiences to create lives that express compassion and caring. I hope that I can make some small contribution to your ability to create and maintain relationships that bring you much love and joy.

Introduction – The Need for New Tools

One of the most curious things I've witnessed during my twenty-six years as a therapist is that almost everyone who comes to me with problems in their relationships thinks that they should already know how to fix things. We seem to think that we emerge from the womb with all the tools we need to successfully relate to each other. When my clients have problems in their relationships, they often feel embarrassed and ashamed. They believe that somehow there is something wrong with them because they don't already know how to make their relationships work, that somehow their lack of skills means that they are inadequate or stupid.

This could not be farther from the truth. As far as I can tell, everyone experiences difficulties in their relationships, more or less, and most of us don't have much of a clue what to do about it. We would never think that we should know how to fix cars or sail a boat without learning from someone with some real skill and experience. These are skills that we need to learn and practice in order to master them. We would never think that we were inadequate or stupid because we didn't know how to sail a boat without first learning how. In many ways, learning how to create and maintain healthy relationships is very much like learning how to repair a car or sail a boat. It requires learning what it takes to be successful, identifying the tools we need to use in order to succeed and how to use these tools.

Now some of you might be thinking, "come on, Alan, give me a break. People have been in relationships since the beginning of time, and anyway, we've all been exposed to people relating to each other in our families since the day we were born." Well, those of you who come from wonderfully healthy and functional families can put this book down now and go read a good novel. The rest of you, though, might want to consider whether the things you've learned are really working as well as you might like them to. Do you really want your parents to serve as the only models for how you want your own relationships to be? I don't. Sure my parents did many things that worked for them, but I want to relate to my wife and children in ways that are healthier and more productive. I want to be able to express my feelings, work out conflicts and create room for everyone to feel appreciated and get what they want out of our relationships. I'm ambitious in my life. I want more than the tools I got from my upbringing can provide. So if you're like me and you want more out of life, wanting to move beyond some of the shortcomings and limitations in past and present relationships, then this book is for you.

In all my years working with people, I've noticed that many of us spend a great deal of time and energy trying to improve our relationships or find better ones. Despite our considerable experience, we can't quite figure out what it takes to create and maintain the healthy partnerships we would like to have. You might wonder why creating and maintaining healthy relationships is such a mystery to us. The answer is revealed when you consider two very important, relatively recent changes. The first is that we have a much greater amount of freedom in relationships. The second is the gradual emergence of emotional intimacy.

The growth of freedom in relationships

The first reason why we find it harder to create and maintain healthy relationships is that we have much more freedom than we have ever had before. Historically, up until very recently, our families and society told us what kinds of relationships we should have and what roles we should play in them. We did what we were supposed to do, fulfilling our sense of obligation and duty to our families and culture by living the roles they picked for us. Unless we took religious vows, society expected us to get married and raise children. Men worked and provided for their families and women reared the children and cared for the home. There was little room for variation. People got married and stayed married because it was the right and almost only thing to do.

This is no longer the case. Society no longer clearly defines the kinds of relationships we can have, and we have a lot more freedom to choose for ourselves. We can choose to get married or not. If we do marry, we can divorce without any social stigma — most of my friends have been divorced, some more than once. We can choose to have children or not, in or out of wedlock. Many married couples choose to remain childless and many have children without getting married. Even our roles if we do marry are no longer clearly defined. Men can choose to stay home to care for their children and women with children can choose to work outside the home, even when they don't need the extra money.

We even have relationships that weren't very common in the past. Men and women can be close friends without being sexually involved with each other. People live together without being married and married people live apart. Then there are all those new kinds of relationships that are created when people with children join up. Children with divorced and remarried parents can have quite a time figuring out how to relate to all their new "relatives". What exactly do you call that kid who is your new stepfather's ex-wife's son from a previous marriage?

So with all these new and different relationships and with no absolute rules about what to do, we really are free to choose for ourselves. Unfortunately, whenever we are faced with new freedoms we also have to deal with new choices and decisions.

The evolution of intimacy

The second reason that we have more difficulty creating and maintaining satisfactory relationships is that most of us seem to have a much greater need for intimacy than our parents did. Our relationships now need to fulfill this extra burden of providing an environment in which we can share who we are and what we're thinking and feeling with each other. I know that I have a greater need to share myself with others and be more involved with their lives than my father did. My children know me more than I knew my father, and I knew him more than he knew his father. My wife and I seem to have more need to talk than our parents did. I've noticed that we're not very different from most of the people in our generation. My brother, like me, is much more involved with his children than my father was with us, and we all seem to be more involved with each other's lives.

In order to understand why our intimacy needs are growing we need to realize that the focus of human evolution has changed. Where in the past, human evolution was largely about our physical evolution as a species, our evolution is now about developing mentally, emotionally and spiritually. Any physical changes we're presently experiencing as a species pale in comparison to our rate of mental, emotional and spiritual growth. Our growth is mainly occurring in these domains of consciousness.

If our present evolution is occurring as a growth in our consciousness, then the form that this increase in consciousness takes is as a growth in our awareness. We are all becoming more and more aware of our thoughts, feelings and spiritual connections. We've become more introspective and less willing to do something in a particular way just because we've always done it that way. Consequently, we now make many of the choices that others used to make for us.

This growth in awareness makes us crave intimacy. Being more aware makes us more sensitive to the isolation we feel whenever we're not connecting with each other. We're more aware of what we think and feel, and we have a much greater need to share what we're experiencing in our attempt to connect with each other.

The need for a new knowledge of relationships

Because of our increased freedom and our greater need for intimacy, the old rules that told us what to do and how to do it are insufficient for the task. These rules emerged in a time of limited possibilities, when intimacy was not as important as doing the right thing through fulfilling our predetermined roles. Consequently, freedom was seriously limited. Rules that rely on people staying married and fulfilling clearly defined roles just don't work in a society with seemingly limitless choices. Our great grandmothers probably wouldn't quite know how to relate to an ex-husband or how to help their children adapt to a new boyfriend.

In the past, the health of our relationships depended on how well we fulfilled certain roles. Now it depends on how well we treat each other. I can remember as a child overhearing my aunt being told by the older women to stop complaining that her husband didn't talk to her. "Count your blessings that you have a husband who brings his paycheck home," they counseled. This is not enough for us. We crave intimacy and are likely to only stay in relationships when we treat each other in ways that feel good.

The problems we now have in creating and maintaining healthy relationships is the legacy of never having had this same degree of freedom and need for intimacy before. Because society limited us to a few, predetermined choices, in the past we didn't need to know how to choose what relationships to be in or what roles to play in them. We didn't even need to know how to sustain a relationship because no one was leaving.

All these new choices and our increased need for intimacy begs a new knowledge of what makes relationships work. We cannot find this knowledge in our past. We must create it by considering how we want our relationships to be and then discovering where our power lies to make a difference in our relationships.

The challenge of freedom is choosing

We can only handle freedom by truly understanding what freedom really is. Being free means that we can choose for ourselves and that we are responsible for our choices. Exercising our freedom means making choices and taking responsibility for them. The young adolescent Tom Hanks character in the movie *Big* discovered when he awoke as an adult that freedom is a two-edged sword. As an "adult", he no longer had parents to make many of his choices for him. Not only did he have to make a lot of decisions, but he also had to figure out what there was to choose. When he brought home a female friend, he discovered that he had choices that were not available to him in his "small" body. Like us, he was learning that in order to make good choices we need to know what our choices are.

Never before have we had to define our choices in relationships because we never before had to do much choosing. Consequently, we mostly don't even know what choices are possible in a relationship. This is our first challenge—defining what our choices are. Without guidance, this challenge is a little like going to a restaurant where before you can choose what to eat you have to decide what to put on the menu, a daunting task. However, this book is designed to provide guidance, defining the choices for you, like a very descriptive and informative menu that helps you to have the best possible dining experience.

Because relationships are more complex, more demanding and occur in an environment of more freedom of choice, we need to define a whole new set of tools to help us with this incredible challenge of making our relationships work. These tools for building healthy, fulfilling relationships are distinctions. In an environment of increased freedom of choice, the tools that will make relationships work are first a set of distinctions that better define the choices available to us, then ways of considering these choices and finally behaviors that will help us practically manifest these choices in our lives.

The power of distinctions

In order to make choices we have to perceive a difference between things. When all things are the same there is no choice. That things are different from each other is what makes it possible to choose. If all foods tasted the same and provided the same nutritional value, then we would have little reason to choose one over another. Without difference, without distinction, there are no choices. Therefore, having choice requires a set of distinctions from which to choose. Distinctions define choice by letting us know what our choices are and sometimes, even that we have choices we can make. Also, more and finer distinctions empower us to make choices that work. Let me share an example with you.

Here in the South, we have little experience with snow. Consequently, our only distinctions about snow, are snowing or not snowing, and ice or no ice. These are not very many distinctions; but this is not a problem for us, because it rarely snows, and when it does we all stay home until it melts. But these limited distinctions about snow would not be enough for Eskimos who live near the Arctic Circle. For much of their year, they have snow of some form or another, and a lot of it. To survive, they need to make numerous decisions based on what kind of snow and snow conditions are present because they just can't wait until it melts. Eskimos have many more distinctions about snow because they need to make important decisions about snowy weather that we in the South never have to make. It's these distinctions that enable them to manage a severe and potentially dangerous environment.

Similarly, in our newly evolved environment of increased freedom and a growing desire for intimacy, we need a whole set of new distinctions that our ancestors didn't have. We need distinctions that will help us navigate this seemingly perilous terrain of relationships, enabling us to make choices and carry them out in ways that will aid us in creating and maintaining healthy, fulfilling relationships.

The importance of distinctions is the behaviors that naturally follow

Without changing our thinking and behavior, distinctions become merely intellectual exercises. Understanding the distinctions in this book without using them to enhance your relationships through action and changes in your attitude is like reading about meditation without actually sitting down to do it. You might gain some intellectual understanding of what meditation is, but you will have no experience of the actual power of the experience.

The power of distinctions about relationships is their ability to influence how we think about and behave in our relationships. For example, in the next chapter, we will distinguish forgiving a behavior from condoning a behavior. This distinction allows us to forgive things without approving of them, so we can get on with our lives together, even after a serious problem. Armed with this distinction, after sharing her feelings with me, my wife can forgive me for having said something mean to her in the middle of an argument. I can then choose to use her feedback to be more thoughtful in the future and learn healthier ways to argue.

Throughout this book I offer clear well-defined, explicit tools for transforming your relationships into ones worth having. You will learn to identify the choices that you have to consider in order to create healthy relationships, how to make good choices and how to think and act in ways that will support your manifesting these choices in your relationships. Because the distinctions throughout the book are universal understandings, you will be able to apply what you learn to all your relationships. You will discover that through simple changes in your thinking and behavior you can work in partnership with others to create and maintain the kind of relationships you really want.

However, before we move on to tools, let me share a brief word about my use of the word partnership in the title of this book. In all honesty, I thought that "Partnership Tools" was a catchier title than "Relationship Tools", but more than that, I want you to think of all relationships as partnerships in which we work together cooperatively to create what we want. Ultimately, building and maintaining healthy relationships is a cooperative endeavor in which we share the responsibility for and hopefully the rewards from what we create together.

Tool #1—Forgiving

Our growing need for intimacy makes forgiving others and ourselves an essential part of all healthy relationships. Being intimate means letting others know what will make our relationships work for us. This then empowers us to care for each other by fully participating in our relationships in an ongoing way.

We create intimacy by sharing the details of our lives with each other. Sharing includes not only what happened, but also how we feel and think about what happened. I create intimacy with my wife by telling her what I wrote about today. Our intimacy deepens as I tell her that I feel good about my writing but I haven't yet decided how to finish this chapter.

Sharing is telling others what's going on in our lives and being heard. Telling my wife about my writing doesn't increase intimacy unless she also hears what I say. If she's too busy dealing with the children or thinking about what happened yesterday or what she has to do tomorrow, then she won't hear me. I might as well go outside and tell it to the moon. To hear me she has to listen to what I say right now; her attention can't be on something else.

My wife and I feel closer when we pay attention to each other. If she tells me how hard her day was, and I'm thinking about what happened yesterday or that she always has a hard time, then I'm not listening to her now. With my attention on past or future events, I'm not being intimate because intimacy can only occur in the present. On the other hand, when my daughter tells me about a basket she wove at school, and I say I can't wait to see it, we both feel closer to each other. Intimacy requires present attention.

The circle of intimacy

Talking and listening are tools that empower us to create and maintain healthy relationships. These tools support an intimacy that will keep all our relationships alive and well. When we share what's going on in our lives, along with our thoughts and feelings about it, we create a potential for closeness. Listening then completes this circle of intimacy by creating a receptive mood

The more we share our innermost thoughts and feelings, the deeper our intimacy. Talking to my mother on the phone about the weather is not as intimate as my mentioning to her that the anniversary of my father's death is approaching. We can be even more intimate when we both share how much we miss him. We feel really close when I tell her how I wish he were here so that he and his granddaughters could know each other. This intimate sharing fosters closeness and a love that will enable us to more easily get through the inevitable hard times we all experience.

Paying attention

The risk in sharing our heartfelt thoughts and feelings with others is that they won't really hear us or reject us when they do. We've all had childhood experiences of not being heard or understood by adults who were too busy or distracted. However, not being aware of how busy they were, we could easily decide that what we had to say wasn't important enough for them to listen. Some of us may even have had the more painful experience of adults verbally rejecting thoughts and feelings as not valid or important. Even as adults these traumatic experiences can still make it difficult for us to share our innermost thoughts and feelings, hesitating to share ourselves for fear of being ignored again.

The greatest gift we can give to those we love is really listening to their heartfelt communications. This, however, requires a skill that society doesn't teach us — paying attention. Because we live in a culture of distraction and the twenty-second sound byte, we need to train ourselves to pay attention to those we love so that we can give them the gift of being heard.

Recently, a friend called and told me that he had just broken up with his girlfriend when he realized that it wasn't working out for him. It would have been easy for me to not make such a big deal about it because he hadn't been with her for very long. But hearing the hurt in his voice, I told him how sorry I was. I could tell that he really appreciated my compassion. This is a man that I have come to love dearly as our relationship has grown closer in the last few years. Throughout this time we've both learned how to truly listen to each other. When I feel upset or blue he's one of the first people I call because I know he'll listen, and when something good happens to me, I want to share this with him as well.

The circle of intimacy is both partners sharing their heartfelt thoughts and feelings and both listening in turn. The quality of our listening depends on our paying attention. Without being heard, the most intimate sharing won't make a bit of difference. Really hearing, however, requires keeping our attention in the present. This can be hard in relationships with history. Past problems and hurts can get in the way of paying attention. Consequently, keeping our attention in the present requires a powerful tool that will help us truly listen to each other. This tool is forgiving.

Forgiving

Recently, I attended my high school reunion. Soon after I got there, a classmate approached me and told me about something I did that really hurt her feelings when we were in grade school together. Every year at school, around the holidays, we each picked a name from a hat and got a gift for that person. That year she picked my name. Her father, who owned a clothing store, suggested that she give me a scarf. But she and her father didn't know that a scarf wasn't a very exciting gift for a ten-year old boy who was hoping for a toy. So when I opened her gift, and she saw the clear disappointment in my face, she was crushed. Because this was a "Secret Santa," she never told me how she felt. Telling me this story twenty years later, she seemed to still be angry with me, as if we were both still ten years old. When I said to her that I didn't remember the incident but could certainly understand how she felt at the time, she seemed to be a little taken aback. It seemed that how she felt now was exactly how she felt back then, expecting me to be the same thoughtless boy I had been back then. Though unfair, this is not unusual. We all make present judgments on past experience, and without doing something to shift our thinking we consistently react to others from our past experience with them.

We all work hard to improve ourselves, to feel better about who we are and to relate to each other in healthier ways. It's not that important that my old schoolmate didn't realize who I've become because we're not involved with each other in any way. But keeping our ongoing relationships healthy requires letting go of the past and bringing our attention to the present. For example, I believe that over the years since our marriage I've learned to be much more considerate of my wife. However, if she failed to recognize this change in me, her experience of me would stay the same no matter what I did. I'd always be the hotheaded man she first met. Fortunately, my wife does pay attention, and she has noticed how much more considerate I've become. The key to her noticing changes I make is her ability to forgive me for past indiscretions.

To maintain healthy, strong relationships we need to forgive others whenever they hurt us. Forgiving means excusing their hurtful behavior without reason. This seems simple, yet it can be extremely hard to forgive even the smallest hurts. Through the remainder of this chapter, we'll consider the benefits of forgiving and examine those misconceptions that stop us from forgiving. Then, we'll learn about four necessary distinctions for forgiving others and ourselves. These are: 1) distinguishing responsibility and self-blame, 2) distinguishing who you are from what you do, 3) distinguishing forgiving from condoning, and 4) distinguishing loving someone and the distance from which you love them.

The Benefits of Forgiving

1. FORGIVING KEEPS OUR ATTENTION IN THE PRESENT

Forgiving returns our attention to the present by putting the past behind us. Forgiving helps us become fully aware of how someone is behaving now. It is the tool that helps us complete an experience, enabling us to move forward in our lives. Without forgiving we would perceive others as they have been, rather than how they are. By forgiving, however, we can move beyond mistakes to reconnect with each other, returning our focus to our long-standing commitments. Let me share an example of how forgiving has worked for me.

Despite the fact that my relationship with my wife is important to me, my actions and words with her can be incredibly thoughtless at times. When I feel bad enough I can do or say hurtful things. Recently, we had a minor crisis, briefly losing one of our dogs, Crystal. After awhile, I began to fear that a car might have hit her out on the road near our house. Feeling upset, I angrily lashed out at my wife and unfairly blamed her for Crystal's being lost. As many people do, I can get irrational when I'm upset, looking to blame others when I suspect that I may have been responsible for a problem.

Eventually, we found Crystal and were greatly relieved; but my wife and I were still in trouble. She was really angry with me, feeling abused by how I had unfairly lashed out at her.

Predictably, I defended myself to her at first, but soon I began to listen to her and I realized what I'd done. Hearing how she felt, I honestly apologized and took responsibility for what I'd unfairly said to her. She accepted my apology and forgave me.

Her act of forgiveness empowered us to leave the incident behind and reconnect with each other. In speaking with her later I learned that she was able to forgive me because she remembered that I had a strong commitment to learn from my mistakes. She trusted that I would use this experience to change in a constructive way. Forgiving me enabled her to return her attention to the present where she could notice that I am gradually learning over time to express my feelings more directly.

Her forgiveness freed me to be able to choose to learn new ways to relate to her in the future. Being forgiven helped me put this incident in the past. There it can serve me as a reference experience for how not to treat her and as a reminder to find better ways to communicate. It also helps me trust that, when I make a mistake in our relationship, I will get another chance to do better.

2. FORGIVING SUPPORTS CHANGE

Forgiving keeps our relationships alive and flexible. It helps us change how we are with each other to fit how we are now, instead of how we've been. In this way, forgiving creates room for change in a relationship.

Forgiving allows us to learn better ways to relate to each other. For example, when my wife and I first met I was a hothead, but I'm learning to express my feelings without losing my temper. I still lose my temper sometimes, but with less intensity and much less frequently. By forgiving my past temper outbursts, my wife creates room in our relationship for me to change. Every time she forgives me, I learn to trust that she will notice when I change, and I feel supported by her. Consequently, her willingness to pay attention and acknowledge my growing ability to communicate better increases my desire to change and please her more.

In contrast to this, if my wife did not forgive me for my past mistakes, she would evaluate changes in my behavior only through the filter of what she already "knows" about me. Strongly believing that I am someone who loses his temper a lot, any changes I make would likely go unnoticed and would have little effect on her opinion of me. No matter how much I changed, she would still think of me as someone with a temper. And without her acknowledgment of the changes in my behavior I would probably just return to my old ways. After all, who wants to work hard to change when it doesn't seem to make a difference?

We can support healthy change in our relationships when we forgive past mistakes and also support new, healthier behaviors. We need to reinforce new behaviors by recognizing and acknowledging them, or they will tend to fade away. If I notice when my older daughter teases her sister but fail to acknowledge when she is considerate of her, she will learn to tease her more because even negative attention is more desired than no attention at all. We all tend to behave in ways that fulfill the expectations that we have for each other. Consider the faithful wife who, repeatedly accused of cheating by her husband, seeks comfort and understanding somewhere else. This turns her husband's unwarranted jealousy into a self-fulfilling prophecy. If I continue to perceive my daughter as inconsiderate of her sister, even though she has made attempts to be more thoughtful, she will stop trying to change because "nobody noticed anyway."

Forgiving prevents our past from shaping our present perception of someone. Unforgiven past mistakes bias our perception of our present situation. Without forgiving me for my past thoughtlessness, my wife would continue to notice when I am thoughtless and not notice or discount when I am thoughtful. In contrast, forgiving my past callous behavior opens her to noticing the positive changes I make.

Whenever we forgive someone, our experience and sense of others matures as they do. Forgiving our loved ones for their past mistakes keeps our relationships up to date and helps us be responsive to their positive changes. Forgiving helps us become more aware of how we are being treated now. It enables us to live in a present that uses the past as a springboard for success instead of a weight that we have to carry.

3. FORGIVING OURSELVES HELPS
US ATTEND TO OTHERS

Forgiving others first requires that we forgive our own mistakes. Forgiving ourselves frees our attention to be more aware of others and potentially more compassionate and responsive to them. It helps us redirect our attention from ourselves and toward others.

When we can't forgive our own mistakes, we can become obsessed with them and consequently have less attention for others. We thus interrupt our natural flow of attention which moves back and forth between others and ourselves. If I don't forgive myself for lashing out at my wife, I can become so obsessed with feeling bad that I don't attend to how what I'm doing now affects her. I'm too busy feeling bad, too wrapped up in myself, to learn from my mistake and change my behavior.

Forgiving requires attention. It requires that we notice what we've done, experience others' reactions to it and learn from our mistakes. To forgive myself I need to first notice how I had unfairly displaced my feelings by lashing out at my wife and then explore my feelings to understand why I did that. I might discover that I felt some personal responsibility for not taking better care of Crystal. Then I can forgive myself and subsequently pay better attention while my wife expresses how it made her feel.

4. WE LEARN FROM OUR MISTAKES

It might seem that those who put a lot of attention on how they treat others, because they don't want to hurt or offend anybody, are being considerate of others. After all, they are constantly checking out whether they have made a mistake, done the right thing or said something stupid. But on closer examination we can see that their attention is really on themselves. They are consumed with how they are doing and how others are reacting to them. They have little attention for what others might need or want because their attention is not on others' needs but on their own need for approval. Ironically, because they don't really pay attention to others, they tend to repeat mistakes, often ensuring that what they most fear actually happens. Consistently out of touch with others, their actions are out of sync with what is happening and sometimes even offensive, and eventually they lose the approval of their friends and colleagues.

This obsession with how they affect others is rooted in their belief that making mistakes is unacceptable and unforgivable. Before we judge them too harshly, though, we need to understand that these people merely represent the extreme of a pattern that most of us share. It's difficult to accept making mistakes and hard to forgive ourselves when we do.

Not being able to accept and forgive our mistakes can drive us to defend ourselves by rationalizing why we did something. We feel compelled to defend ourselves so we can excuse what we did. When we're late for an appointment, we always have a good reason for our delay. If I forget someone's birthday, it was because I was so busy.

Without forgiving, when we can't successfully defend our mistakes, we punish ourselves for what failures we are. We condemn ourselves by admitting how awful and inadequate we truly are. We feel bad about ourselves and express our low self-esteem in a barrage of self-criticism. "I am so stupid. I can't believe how ignorant I am. I'm such an idiot." Eventually, this self-criticism keeps us from relating to others because we're too busy beating up on ourselves. Constant self-criticism focuses our attention on ourselves and away from others, becoming the most extreme form of self-involvement.

A strong example of this pattern is those people who take responsibility for everything that happens around them. These are the people who apologize to me when I step on their toe. They are the people who worry about whether they said the right thing to someone in mourning instead of attending to how the mourner is doing.

In contrast, when we forgive ourselves we only have to attend to mistakes long enough to learn from them. When I forgive myself for lashing out at my wife, I only need to learn enough from the experience to be different in the future. Forgiving our mistakes and moving through them helps us redirect our attention to the present where we can focus on others as well as ourselves. Forgiving, we can attend to our relationships and the important work of forgiving those we love for their mistakes. Here is a graphic summary of the benefits of forgiving.

The Benefits of Forgiving

1. Keeps our attention in the present
2. Creates room for change
3. Helps us attend to others instead of only ourselves
4. Gives us the freedom to make and learn from our mistakes

A myth that gets in the way

Learning how to forgive ourselves requires understanding the obstacles we place in our way, how we stop ourselves from forgiving. If we find it hard to forgive, we either see some danger in forgiving, or we believe that not forgiving serves us in some way, or both. As it happens, both these stumbling blocks to forgiving are rooted in a popular myth — that the way to be responsible for our mistakes is to blame ourselves. We've learned to beat ourselves up when we make mistakes, thinking that will help us avoid repeating our mistakes. Considering this belief, the best way for me to stop lashing out at my wife unfairly is to beat myself up for having done so. The problem is that this strategy doesn't work. It only perpetuates the problem. Let me share with you how self-blame actually makes us repeat mistakes over and over again.

How equating self-blame and responsibility stops us from forgiving

The first misunderstanding that stops us from forgiving ourselves is that self-blame is the same as responsibility. If this were the case then, in order to be responsible for our mistakes, we have to blame ourselves for them.

When I equate self-blame with responsibility, in order to take responsibility for my mistake of lashing out at my wife, I have to blame myself. Following this reasoning, if I want to continue to be responsible, I cannot forgive myself because forgiving myself means letting go of blame, which, with self-blame and responsibility being the same, also means letting go of responsibility. In a nutshell, we blame ourselves because we think self-blame makes us responsible; but in actuality self-blame only leads to our becoming irresponsible. Let me explain how this works.

When I equate self-blame with responsibility, if I stop blaming myself for lashing out at my wife, I also stop being responsible for what I did. I can only remain responsible by continuing to blame myself. By the same token, if I stop blaming myself, I become irresponsible and therefore more likely to repeat my mistakes.

However, hanging on to self-blame in order to avoid being irresponsible is a little like drinking arsenic to kill the flu. I might kill the virus, but overall my stomach will feel worse. Self-blame might help us act responsibly for a while, but eventually self-blame leads to our being irresponsible. This is because self-blame feels bad. So for as long as I blame myself, staying responsible for what I did, I continue to feel bad. Therefore, the only way to feel better, when I equate self-blame with responsibility, is to let go of self-blame and become irresponsible. My choice is to let go of self-blame (and responsibility) or to continue to feel bad for what I did.

Feeling bad is no fun, and after a while I've had enough and grow weary of feeling bad. Unfortunately, as long as I need to blame myself in order to remain responsible, I continue to feel bad. I can only feel better when I let go of blaming myself. However, I won't consciously do this because I want to stay responsible. Therefore, the only way to feel better is to unconsciously block out my awareness, creating amnesia for having unfairly lashed out at my wife. When I forget what I did, I can stop blaming myself and I feel better.

Unfortunately, when I block my awareness of what I've done, I also let go of my responsibility for it. Thus I become irresponsible, which is what I was trying to avoid by blaming myself in the first place. Ironically, the end result of hanging onto self-blame in order to stay responsible is eventually getting tired of feeling bad and forgetting about it, thus becoming irresponsible and much more likely to repeat my mistake. We've all known people like this who are great at beating themselves up for making mistakes and even better at repeating their mistakes.

When we equate self-blame with responsibility, it's impossible to be responsible and learn from our mistakes without feeling bad. When we learn that responsibility is distinct from self-blame, we can stop blaming ourselves and continue to take responsibility for our mistakes. But how do we make this distinction?

When We Equate Self-blame with Responsibility

a mistake is made

self-blame	no self-blame
⬇	⬇
feel bad	irresponsibility
⬇	⬇
block awareness, self blame and bad feelings	repeat mistake
⬇	
irresponsibility	
⬇	
repeat mistake	

The nature of forgiving: distinguishing between self-blame and responsibility

Now that we know the benefits of forgiving our mistakes and see how self-blame actually leads to repeating our mistakes, we are ready to understand the true nature of forgiving. Forgiving our mistakes requires the realization that responsibility is distinct from self-blame. Only by distinguishing between responsibility and self-blame can we let go of self-blame while retaining responsibility for our actions. The two keys to realizing this distinction are separating the doer from the deed and accepting that making mistakes is an important part of being successful in life.

DISTINGUISHING THE DOER FROM THE DEED

When we make mistakes, blaming ourselves implies that because we have done something bad, we, ourselves, are bad. In contrast, taking responsibility implies that we are responsible for our actions but that a mistake does not make us bad. Blame goes beyond responsibility by insisting that we identify with our actions. We can represent this difference in this way:

blame = responsibility + identifying with the mistake

Subsequently, when we let go of identifying with our mistakes, we are left with the following equation:

blame - identifying with the mistake = responsibility

Distinguishing responsibility from blame in this way acknowledges the difference between who we are and what we do. It differentiates between the doer and the deed. We are human beings who can and do make mistakes; we are not the mistakes themselves. In the example from my own life, without distinguishing self-blame from responsibility, along with being responsible for lashing out at my wife, I would think that I was an awful person for doing such a thing. In contrast, by distinguishing who I am from what I do, I can take responsibility for mistreating her without feeling that I'm an awful person for it.

THE DIFFERENCE BETWEEN FORGIVING AND CONDONING

Many of us won't forgive because we fail to realize that forgiving something does not mean that we approve of it. When we distinguish the doer from the deed we can forgive someone without condoning what he or she did. Condoning implies that we find their mistake in some way acceptable, that we approve of what happened. When we forgive, we don't necessarily approve of what happened. Actually, if we did approve, we would have nothing to forgive.

When I forgive myself for lashing out at my wife I'm not condoning my behavior. When my wife forgives me for lashing out at her she is not telling me that she approves of my behavior. She's only telling me that she's willing to believe in me and give me the chance to learn from my mistake.

ACCEPTING MAKING MISTAKES

The second difference between self-blame and responsibility is that, while self-blame is rooted in believing that mistakes are bad and unacceptable, responsibility accepts mistakes as a natural part of being human. When we make a mistake, being responsible only requires that we accept what has happened and take ownership for what we contributed to the mistake. We don't prefer making mistakes, but when a mistake happens we accept it without insisting that we feel bad. When we're responsible, we only need to admit what we've done and commit ourselves to learning from our mistakes.

Consequently, self-blame feels different from responsibility. When we're not okay with making mistakes, our mistakes feel bad because they are unacceptable. We can represent this distinction in this way:

$$\text{Blame} = \text{Responsibility} + \text{feeling bad}$$

$$(\text{by not accepting our mistakes})$$

On the other hand, the more we accept the human inevitability of making mistakes, the more we feel okay in spite of our mistakes. When we accept our mistakes we transform self-blame into responsibility:

$$\text{Blame} - \text{feeling bad} = \text{Responsibility}$$

The importance of making mistakes

There's a story about a famous Zen archer, who when an admirer approached and asked what made it possible for him to hit the bulls-eye with every shot, replied, "The thousand times I missed." He recognized that mistakes allow us to learn. In order to forgive ourselves we must accept the necessity of making mistakes in the natural course of living. Mistakes are a normal and very important part of life. If we don't accept mistakes, we lose the benefit that we gain from making them.

Mistakes are an important part of all learning and progress. We do better in life when we are willing to learn from our mistakes. Also, when we're not willing to make mistakes, we don't take the risks that go with venturing into new areas of experience. Experience is the great teacher, and our experience is not complete without making mistakes.

Our attitude about mistakes, not mistakes themselves, inhibits our learning and progress. Avoiding mistakes at all costs because they're unacceptable keeps us from exploring unfamiliar areas of learning and experience. The greatest discoveries occur in environments where we respect mistakes as an important part of learning. Thomas Edison tried hundreds of types of filaments for his light bulbs before he found one that worked.

Without a willingness to make mistakes, progress and personal evolution would be extremely slow if not impossible. We need to honor mistakes as an important part of every learning process. When I learned to ice skate as an adult, my friends told me that I wouldn't progress if I either fell all the time or not at all. They said I was on track only when I challenged myself enough to sometimes fall. Accepting making mistakes while not identifying with them is an important part of our learning how to succeed in life.

Changing cultural support for feeling bad about mistakes

The insistence in our culture that we feel bad about mistakes is rooted in the false belief that this is the only way we can motivate ourselves to change. We're afraid that if we don't feel bad about a mistake we won't have the motivation, or even desire, to get it right the next time. Thinking in this way, we learn to punish our children when they make mistakes so that they will be motivated to do better. As we grow into adults, however, we no longer need to be punished by others for our mistakes, because we've learned to do it to ourselves through guilt.

Even though behavioral psychologists tell us that reward is much more effective than punishment in shaping behavior, we insist on punishing ourselves for our mistakes by feeling guilty for what we've done. Many religions teach us to feel guilty for our sins, using repentance as a measure of our devotion. Consequently, we learn on very deep levels that self-blame and guilt will lead to improvement and even redemption.

This way of thinking fails to recognize that we are compassionate beings who can recognize how we affect others and that our need for intimacy is strong enough motivation to work on improving our relationships. We don't need to feel bad to motivate ourselves to change. As long as we are sensitive to how our behavior and communication affect others, and we can own our strong desire for intimacy, then there's no reason for us to feel guilty for our mistakes. Also, as I described in the previous section in this chapter, feeling guilty actually gets in the way of positive change and pretty much guarantees that we will repeat our mistakes. On the other hand, as long as we recognize our mistakes and take responsibility for learning from them, we have no need to feel bad.

Creating an environment where mistakes are accepted

Communicating about our mistakes requires that we create an environment where we see mistakes as a natural part of life. This is not to say that we prefer mistakes, but we accept them when they happen. Relationships are learning processes, and mistakes are an important part of learning. Avoiding mistakes at all costs gets in the way of the progress that comes with learning from them.

We can learn that mistakes are a normal part of life by talking about them. Talking about an experience takes the power out of it, especially when the listeners are supportive and loving. Sharing how our families of origin handled mistakes can release bottled up emotions and lead to healing. When we share we get the opportunity to both give and receive compassion and understanding

When I was young my father could never admit that he had made a mistake. When he did make a mistake, we just didn't discuss it and acted as if nothing had happened. On the other hand, if someone else made a mistake, my father would often get very upset and angry about it. Obviously, mistakes were not acceptable in his family. In turn, I absorbed the message that it wasn't okay to make mistakes. Consequently, I spent a great deal of energy trying to succeed and avoiding situations where it was possible that I might not. Using my father as a model, I also learned to be impatient with others' mistakes.

With help from my wife, I now live in a family where we try our best to be accepting and forgiving of mistakes. At times I still find myself not wanting to admit that I made a mistake, but given time I can take responsibility for what I've done. Even though I'm still impatient at times when my wife or one of my daughters makes a mistake, I've learned to admit my mistake of impatience and apologize for not being more supportive.

Over the years my wife and I have become familiar with the ways that each of our families of origin dealt with mistakes. Sharing our stories with each other has helped us better understand how we each got to be the way that we are. This helps us be more compassionate, patient and forgiving of each other. Becoming more aware of how we learned to respond to mistakes has helped us create a more accepting and forgiving family environment

This kind of discussion creates an environment of mutual support that works toward solution instead of blame. It's courageous to make ourselves vulnerable enough to share our innermost feelings and thoughts. But the payoff of greater understanding and intimacy is well worth the risk.

Failing to distinguish between self-blame and responsibility is like throwing out the baby (responsibility) with the bath water (self-blame). Conversely, when we realize that self-blame is different and distinct from responsibility, we can let go of self-blame and remain responsible for our mistakes. Once we understand this distinction, forgiveness is the most useful response to mistakes. We forgive ourselves, letting go of self-blame and guilt, and retain responsibility for our actions. Taking responsibility for our actions, without feeling bad or identifying with them, allows us to be aware of what we've done while continuing to learn and grow from them.

Forgiving others

Not forgiving others is costly. When we don't forgive others, our relationships fail to evolve, because without forgiving it's impossible to recognize and respond to the positive changes that others make. Unforgiven events are like rocks that narrow the passage of a river, creating a great current through which navigation becomes increasingly more difficult. In such tricky waters, when no one acknowledges our changes, we lose hope for changing and improving our relationships. Without hope for change, we're left with the survival of the relationship as our only concern. Also, in relationships without forgiving we see others' attempts to improve our relationships through the filters of unforgiven, past events. Without forgiving me my wife would still think of me as someone with a temper, even after years without angry outbursts.

Forgiving is essential to a healthy relationship. When we forgive we are clearing away obstructions that inhibit the natural flow of the relationship. Things slow down, giving us the space and time to thoughtfully deal with the problems that naturally arise in any healthy relationship.

Judgment and forgiving

All human beings are prone to judge — it's a mechanism that has contributed to our survival as a species. Beside ourselves, we're most likely to judge those who are closest to us because their actions are most likely to affect us. Even though learning to not judge others and ourselves can be extremely difficult, we can use forgiveness to move beyond our judgments and preserve our relationships.

When we judge what someone has done or said and fail to move beyond judgment to forgiveness, we freeze our relationship at a certain point in time. Our judgment turns the movie of a relationship into a still-frame image that's fixed and lifeless. In contrast, forgiving breathes vitality into our relationships by acknowledging that mistakes happen and thus empowers us to move forward.

To never judge or evaluate is an ideal, but it is not a solution. Some of us may think that we make no judgments, freely accepting all that others do and say, but if we're human and breathing, we judge. Thinking that we don't judge others is only a way of fooling ourselves so our judgments flow under the surface of our awareness, sneaking up on us to run our lives without our knowing it. We end up acting out our judgments without the chance to acknowledge and move beyond them. The only alternative to letting our judgments run our lives is forgiving.

How forgiving others is similar to forgiving ourselves

Forgiving others is in many ways similar to forgiving ourselves. We can forgive others when we distinguish the difference between blame and responsibility by accepting the inevitability of making mistakes and separating the doer from the deed. We can forgive others for any wrong they may have done to us and still hold them responsible for their actions. Forgiving others is not condoning what they did but accepting that people make mistakes. It gives them the space to learn from their mistakes without the stigma of being identified with them.

The issue of trust

Even when we transform blame into responsibility, sometimes we still find it hard to trust others. Because we have no control over whether they will learn from their mistakes and change, we must depend on their ability to be forgiving of themselves. All we can do by forgiving others is create room for them to forgive themselves. We have no guarantee that they will. When my wife forgave me for lashing out at her, she made room for me to forgive myself. But she had no way of knowing that I would use that space to learn from my mistake. There's always the danger that, despite her forgiving me, I would not be able to forgive myself, languish in self-blame until I couldn't stand it any longer and block the experience. This would clear the way for irresponsibly repeating my mistake.

This dilemma is a problem only in ongoing relationships. Whether the driver who cut me off on the freeway today learns from his mistake has little effect on my life. However, we feel less inclined to forgive those who are close to us because we fear that they might repeat their mistakes, causing further damage to our relationships. This explains how it can sometimes be harder to forgive relatives than to forgive strangers.

Consider the woman whose husband has been verbally abusive to her in front of her family. Because she felt great hurt and embarrassment, she wonders whether to forgive him. If she forgives him, she makes herself vulnerable to further hurt and injury. On the other hand, if she doesn't forgive him, she creates a static relationship by filtering everything that happens in the future through her hurt from the past. This leaves little possibility that he will be able to change in ways that will be noticed or acknowledged.

It also increases the probability that he will repeat his verbal abuse because he will feel hurt and angry that he wasn't acknowledged when he did try to change. The question then is how can we create relationships where we can trust each other to change and avoid this dilemma of being stuck between our fear of being vulnerable and our desire to be supportive.

Creating trusting relationships

Creating trusting relationships requires talking about our mistakes. Our mistakes point out what we need to change, and changing our response to our mistakes requires that we talk about them.

How we feel about our mistakes determines how easily we talk about them. If we believe that they are unacceptable, we'll hesitate to discuss our mistakes. If in our past people reacted negatively to our mistakes, we learned to hide them. We may even have learned to avoid talking about others' mistakes, sparing them the painful guilt and embarrassment of admitting that they made a mistake.

When we share that we have made a mistake, we let those we care about know that we are responsible for our actions. They don't have to become watchdogs for our behavior because we are paying attention to how we affect others. In this way we create a trusting and forgiving environment in which together we handle the mistakes we make, and where none of us is bad for making them. Recognizing and owning our mistakes becomes the rich ground for growing healthier relationships. Communicating better, we become aware of each other's concerns and wishes, grow to trust each other's ability to learn from mistakes and become empowered to successfully handle any future problems that arise.

Trusting that others will learn from their mistakes

Trusting that others will learn from their mistakes and be counted on to change becomes easier when we realize that most mistakes aren't particularly serious or life threatening. No one ever died from hurt feelings or personal offense. As adults, only mistakes that threaten us physically are dangerous. We can learn to trust more easily when we consciously distinguish situations that are life threatening and physically dangerous from those that aren't. We can relax when we realize that the risk of being hurt emotionally is much less dangerous than risks that involve physical danger. My wife will not die if I forget her birthday, but she might die if I play with a loaded gun in front of her.

We also must distinguish those situations that have the potential to emotionally damage children from those that affect only adults. We need to shelter children emotionally, while adults can usually take care of themselves. Making these distinctions, we are now ready to learn how to trust that others will learn from their mistakes and change.

Trusting others really means trusting our own ability to discern whom we can count on in a particular situation and whom we can't. When my wife trusts me to learn from my mistake, she is really trusting her assessment that I am someone who will choose to learn. However, there's never any guarantee that we're right. When we trust we're always taking the risk of being hurt again, but even if we're hurt again, we only need to forgive ourselves for mistakenly trusting, and go on. Eventually we'll learn whom to trust.

Sometimes I've trusted others and been disappointed, but I was able to learn from my mistakes. On the other hand, most of the time that I've trusted others, when I communicated well and fully, their subsequent behavior supported my trusting them.

Distinguishing love from proximity

In a perfect world, in addition to forgiving all mistakes, we would all acknowledge our mistakes, take responsibility for them and learn from them. However, we don't live in a perfect world. Sometimes no matter how compassionate and forgiving we are, some people are not willing or able to change. When we are the subjects of repeated abuse, for example, we have the right to leave that abusive situation. Getting away from an abusive situation can range from taking some time and space to think things through to ending a relationship without further contact. We have the right to step back and protect ourselves from abuse.

Unfortunately, many of us find it hard to step back from those we love and care about because we confuse the fact that we love someone with being physically close and emotionally involved with them. We believe that, if we love someone, we have to want to be close to him or her, and that we can only move away from them if we no longer love them. When we believe that we can't continue to love someone and also move away from them, we can't move away until we stop loving. This means that we must endure an abusive situation until it destroys our love because the only way we can protect ourselves is to stop loving.

Sometimes, people use the words, "if you loved me, you wouldn't leave" to keep a spouse or child nearby. A woman in an abusive relationship lives in a world where she has to love less or not at all in order to take care of herself.

The solution lies in learning that love is not the same as physical closeness and emotional involvement. I love my cat, Bonnie, who loves to sleep in my lap when I'm reading. I also love the lion at the zoo, but safely from behind the barrier. Whether to love someone is a separate decision from how closely involved we want to be with him or her. Each of us has the right to choose from what distance we want to love someone. We have the right to take the space we need to protect ourselves and continue to love, becoming less involved with those who treat us poorly and whom we no longer trust. We can even choose to become less involved with someone because our interests have diverged, feeling no guilt because we know that we still love and care for them.

Leaving abusive relationships is actually a loving act. It involves loving others because it gives them feedback that they wouldn't get if we stayed. When we've tried every way we know to give feedback while still close and involved, leaving can be the feedback that makes others take the problem seriously. We're doing what we can to help the change. Leaving abusive situations is also loving of ourselves because we say that we're no longer willing to receive abuse, that we need to be treated better. In contrast, staying with those who are abusive and unchanging can give the message that the situation is okay with us. Sometimes, leaving is the only way to keep our love alive.

Keeping our hearts open

Learning how to step back while keeping our hearts open is a great challenge in a culture that believes stepping back means you've stopped loving. However, learning to step back with our hearts open means that we never have to close our hearts to someone. We can choose less intimate involvement with others and still love them and care about them. When we can recognize that loving and the distance from which we love are distinct, we have the power to take care of ourselves while continuing to be fully compassionate and loving. We are free to choose to love in a way that works for us.

Distinguishing when we are truly keeping our hearts open from when we are just mentally embracing the idea of keeping our hearts open is difficult. It seems, however, that keeping our hearts open is not an idea or mental process, but a state of being that has distinctive personal feelings associated with it. Being able to forgive is a good indication that our hearts are still open. Another indication is if we can feel good when those who have hurt us succeed in their lives, regardless of how it affects us.

Whether to stay in a relationship and keep "trying" or to leave is a personal decision. There is never an absolutely "right" or "wrong" choice. But whatever we choose, we need to take responsibility for our choice and the ramifications of our choice, whether we anticipated them or not. Whether we choose to stay close and involved or leave and disengage, we can try to forgive all others and ourselves.

Forgiving in action

As you begin to understand and integrate these distinctions about forgiving you will feel more able to forgive. At this point you are ready to move forgiving from the abstract realm of understanding into your own direct experience. Forgiving as mere philosophy will fail. It will succeed only as an ongoing practice. Forgiving occurs moment by moment. Fortunately, the more we practice, the easier it becomes. The practice of forgiving reminds us of children who love everyone they meet. They don't need a philosophy of love. They are love.

When we are able to forgive others, we are empowering those we love to become the kind of people that they really want to be. All people want to love, and when we forgive others for their mistakes, they feel loved and cared for and can move beyond their limitations. They, in turn, can fulfill their own desire to be fully loving to those they love. In this way forgiving empowers us to live together in an environment of mutual love and trust.

Important Distinctions About Forgiving

1. Responsibility is different from self-blame.

2. The doer and the deed are distinct.

3. Accepting mistakes does not mean preferring mistakes.

4. Forgive does not mean condone.

5. Whether to love, and the distance from which to love, are separate decisions.

Tool #2—Making Requests

Michael and Deborah are in their mid-thirties. After living together for three years, they are dealing with all the questions about marriage, commitment and children that come with their age. They feel pressured to make some decision about their future together, and even though they love each other, lately they've been arguing more. Deborah thinks Michael would make a good father if he would just make a few changes. She feels that he's presently too inconsiderate and self-centered to give their children everything they would need. The last time they discussed marriage and children, she shared her concerns with Michael, but he felt attacked, defended himself and withdrew. Michael thinks that Deborah is too serious all the time. Whenever he teases her about how serious she is, she becomes depressed and quiet. She tells her best friend that she feels inadequate, that she can't give Michael what he wants. They've both thought about breaking up, but the nagging feeling that there is something else they could do stops them.

When I ask people why they complain to someone they care about, they most often reply that they're only trying to improve their relationship. So behind their complaining is the good intention of improving their relationships, and they complain about whatever they believe keeps their relationships from working. The wife who complains to her husband that he doesn't spend enough time with her merely wants him to spend time with her. The friend who complains that you don't call enough just wants you to call more. Unfortunately, all complaining seems to create is a lot of bad feelings.

What happens when we complain

Whether or not we get what we want, complaining doesn't help relationships. Even when others submit to our complaints, they will resent having to change in order to please us. They feel coerced into changing and unappreciated for who they are. They may even feel that there is something wrong with them and that in order to be okay they have to change something about themselves. Feeling bad in this way does not foster healthy relationships.

The problem with complaining is that it doesn't work. Instead of improving our relationships, it usually makes them worse. Even when we've created a loving environment through forgiving, complaining can easily sabotage the trust we've built. Like Michael and Deborah, when someone complains to us that we've done something wrong or not done enough, we feel inadequate and criticized by them. Instead of improving relationships, complaints alienate us, making us want to distance ourselves from each other. After all, who wants to be close to someone who is constantly pointing out our shortcomings to us?

Complaining usually doesn't get people to change. When we feel criticized, we often feel too defensive to want to change and too bad about ourselves to be resourceful enough to change. Complaining can even reinforce the behavior that we want changed. For example, Michael's complaint that Deborah was too serious only made her become more serious and worried about their relationship.

Sometimes, when we complain and nothing changes, we continue to complain. This continual complaining eventually turns into nagging, and nagging doesn't work. People don't like to be nagged, nor do they like to nag.

Though it may seem that some people enjoy nagging, almost every time I've taught a chronic nagger other ways of effectively communicating, their nagging subsided.

Another response to our complaining not working is to stop complaining. But simply giving up our complaints is also ineffective because we usually give up by withdrawing. When someone doesn't respond to our complaints, we can feel that our needs and desires aren't important to them and then withdraw to lick our wounds. Everyone's left feeling inadequate and incapable of doing anything to help the relationship. Feeling alienated and alone, we move closer to the edge that is "falling out of love."

Why complaining doesn't work

There are several reasons why complaining doesn't work. First, complaining directs attention to the problems in a relationship and ignores what is actually working and good about a relationship. When Deborah tells Michael that he's too self-centered and inconsiderate, she fails to tell him the things she appreciates about him. Second, complaining offers no solutions. Deborah's complaint about Michael doesn't address what she would like him to do instead. Even if he responded to her complaint, he wouldn't be sure what he could do to improve things. Third, by directing attention toward the problem and not the solution, complaining focuses our attention on the past rather than the present and future. Deborah's complaint is about what Michael has done wrong not about what he could do in the future to improve their relationship.

By failing to offer solutions and focusing on the past, complaining does little to insure that we'll get what we want. Focusing on what we don't want instead of what we want, complaining is like telling your travel agent that you want to go to St. Louis by saying that you hated Chicago on your last vacation. Eventually you're wondering how you ended up with tickets to Detroit.

Another problem with complaining is how we complain. When we complain, we usually speak in a blaming and accusatory manner. Because blaming doesn't separate the doer from the deed, we hear complaints as statements about who we are. Thus we take complaints personally, hearing them as "I'm wrong to have done this," instead of "I have done something that someone I care about doesn't like." Ironically, in those instances when we do change in response to a complaint, others can perceive our changed behavior as the admission that we're wrong. Changing in response to a blaming complaint justifies it, supporting the notion that we've been bad. No wonder we're rarely willing to change in response to complaining.

Complaining also makes us feel separate and alienated, eroding our sense of togetherness and cooperation. It's hard to feel that you're on the same side as people who repeatedly criticize your behavior. The more they criticize you, the more you feel alienated from them and the more you want to get away from them. Eventually, even being with them can become a stimulus for thinking about your shortcomings and feeling bad about yourself. Children whose parents constantly complain about them can't wait to move. Networks have made a lot of money portraying people trying to get away from their critical mothers-in-law on TV. This is funny on TV, but maybe not so much in real life. Complaining separates people, when what we really need and want is to work together to create better relationships.

Finally, because of how our minds work, even the language of a complaint supports our repeating behaviors that attract complaints. To help you understand the importance of language let me offer a hypothetical example in which I say to my daughter, "Your room is too messy." When I tell her that her room is too messy, in order for my daughter to mentally process my complaint, she has to think about her messy room. This is like being asked to not think of elephants, right now. Of course, to consider this request we must think about elephants. Try it out. Try to not think of elephants, right now...you think of elephants. Therefore, when I tell my daughter that her room is too messy, she thinks of her messy room. Without also talking to her about cleaning her room, it's likely that she'll *only* think about her messy room. Consequently, if you believe as I do that most behavior is unconscious and automatic, we can accurately predict that pointing out to my daughter that her room is messy will reinforce keeping it messy and do little towards getting it clean. After hearing that her room is messy, as soon as her conscious attention drifts, the thought of her messy room will flow into her unconscious, and this is as good as hypnotizing her and giving her the suggestion to keep her room messy.

Our minds do not process negative thoughts. They think only in positive frames. Asking a child to stop dragging his feet almost always ensures his continuing to do it. As soon as his attention moves to something else, which happens every few seconds in young children, the thought in his unconscious mind is to drag his feet. The solution is to request that he lift his feet when walking. This solution seems pretty straightforward, but before I discuss making requests let me address a concern you might have about giving up complaining.

Keeping our complaints to ourselves

You might be wondering how it's possible to deal with the problems in our relationships without complaining. This is a valid concern. However, recognizing that there's a difference between what we think and what we say aloud resolves this concern. A wise friend once suggested to me that I didn't have to express every thought I had. I respectfully listened to her advice and subsequently I have attempted to follow it ever since with very positive results in my life. If Michael were to follow this advice, he could recognize that he doesn't like how serious Deborah is being without complaining to her, as long as he also invites her to change by making requests in the respectful way described later in this chapter.

Without doubt, identifying the problems in our relationships is important to their health and success. However, communicating our problems out loud in the form of a complaint is never necessary. There are much better ways to get the changes we want.

How requests are better than complaints

Talking about problems is unnecessary when we communicate what we want to have happen instead. We don't need to complain when we can request what we want. Instead of complaining to your best friend that she doesn't call you enough, you can request that you'd like her to call more often. In the example with my daughter, I might request that she clean her room instead of telling her that her room is messy.

Requests solve many of the problems inherent in complaints. They direct our attention away from what's wrong in a relationship by being solution-centered rather than problem-centered, while addressing what we want to happen in the future instead of dwelling on the past.

Requests enhance everyone's sense of self worth. Making requests means that we're *asking* someone to do something for us, so they get to choose because we're only asking them, not telling them. When we make requests instead of complaints, we're acknowledging that their concerns and priorities are also important to us. Your request that your friend call more is letting her know what you think could improve your relationship. Subsequently she can consider how your request fits in with the rest of her life and then decide how she wishes to respond. Even if she declines your request, she knows that your relationship is important to you, creating an opening for future communication.

We all have different priorities. If having her room clean is more important to me than it is to my daughter, she'll probably refuse my request. However, my request does open a dialogue between us which might lead to a better understanding of each other. Talking will help us create feelings of closeness and cooperation that are in sharp contrast to the feelings of separation and alienation that complaining creates.

Requests are easier to hear than complaints because requests address what someone wants from us without criticizing what we're doing. When I complain to my daughter about her messy room, she can easily hear this as criticism. She's less likely to feel criticized when I ask her to clean her room because I'm asking for what I want, not evaluating her behavior.

Because they are positive statements, requests acknowledge that both our conscious and unconscious thoughts shape what we do. Stating things positively, for example, asking your friend to call more, insures that when her conscious attention moves to something else, as it will, her unconscious will retain the thought of calling more. Consequently, she'll find it easier to honor your request. When I request that my daughter clean her room, and she agrees, even if her attention wanders, unconsciously she retains the idea of a cleaner room and may actually do those things that will keep her room clean.

Comparing Complaints and Requests

Complaints	Requests
1. Make others feel bad and less resourceful	1. Enhance self worth
2. Push people away	2. Are inclusive
3. Focus on problems	3. Focus on solutions
4. Keep our attention in the past	4. Direct attention to the future
5. Seem personal to the receiver	5. Are personal to the sender

How to make requests

The two greatest challenges when making requests are minimizing blame and fostering an environment of cooperation and shared responsibility. Others will want to honor our requests when they feel respected and know that we're willing to help. In addition, how we state our requests can greatly influence how others hear them.

Requests concern what someone is doing, not their value as a person. Therefore, our requests must clearly state that we want someone to change their behavior, not themselves. For example, my request to my daughter would be to clean her room, not to become a cleaner person. This helps us keep what she does distinct from who she is. Asking your best friend to call more is better than asking her to "be a good friend."

Requests aren't commands or orders. Requests ask others to do something instead of telling them to do it. Commands are disrespectful. Commanding my daughter to "go clean your room" implies that what I want is more important than the reasons that my daughter might have for not wanting to clean her room. It also leaves little room for negotiation which can lead to a power struggle that has little or nothing to do with cleaning her room.

Because requests are solely about what we want, we need to state them in a way that reflects this. Requests in the form of simple statements or questions are best. A request in the form of a simple statement to my daughter could be "I would like you to clean your room." This simply states what I want, saying nothing about my daughter as a person or her behavior up till now. The same request in the form of a question might be "Would you be willing to clean up your room?" This also merely addresses what I want, not who she is or what she's done before.

Both statements about what we want and questions about what others are willing to do respect their right to choose, direct and be responsible for their own lives and behavior. Each leaves room for discussion and negotiation without sinking into power struggles or questioning others' values or right to their own preferences. Making requests in the form of questions or statements respects that differing wants and priorities are often the case and not a problem.

We can help others fulfill our requests by using positive language. For example, telling my daughter that I'd like her to stop being so messy sounds like a request, but it's really a clandestine complaint about her room being messy. It's the proverbial wolf in sheep's clothing, a complaint (the wolf) pretending to be a request (the sheep). In contrast, a true request would be telling her that I'd like her to clean her room.

Because reasons are purely subjective, everyone usually has good reasons for their requests. For example, I might want my daughter to clean her room today because some friends are coming or because we're showing the house to prospective buyers. On the other hand, I might just be a little neurotic about cleanliness. So sharing our reasons for a request does not justify our request. However, sharing our reasons for our requests does let others know why something is important to us. By letting others know why we want something, we include them in our lives, thus sharing ourselves in a mood of cooperation.

Others will feel more inclined to honor our requests when we share our reasons for making the request first and then the request itself. Framing our requests this way will help affect the response we get. If I start by asking my daughter to clean her room without telling her why it's important to me, you can bet that she probably won't hear anything that I say after that. This is particularly true if I'm making a request in a touchy area. In contrast, she's more likely to hear my request to clean her room if I first tell her the reasons for my request. Let me share an example from my practice of how the order in which a client communicated what he wanted to his daughter significantly affected her response.

My client began a session by describing a conversation in which his college age daughter mentioned to him that she wanted to study in Paris the next summer. His first response was to question her about where she would stay and with whom, and if she knew anyone in Paris. Predictably, his daughter got extremely angry, leaving in a huff as she said over her shoulder, "Just forget it! I won't go."

He was still upset about it the next day in my office. He told me that he didn't want her to be angry with him, but he didn't know what to do. I began by asking him how he felt about her going to Paris that summer. He said that of course he wanted her to go, but that he also felt concerned for her safety while she was there. I suggested that he call her, *begin* by stating that he wanted her to go, and then state his concern about her safety — the positive intention behind the grilling. He thought this was good advice and promised to call his daughter immediately following our session. At our next session, he walked in with a beaming smile on his face. He reported that his daughter was indeed going to Paris with his blessing and support. After saying what I had coached him to say to her, his daughter reported that she already had well thought out plans, including a place to stay with friends, a course of study and a telephone number where he could reach her. Consequently, he felt secure about her safety, she felt supported and, more importantly, their relationship was back on track.

In addition to stating our reasons for a request, it's important that we share what we think honoring our requests will do for us. This creates the possibility of getting our needs met in ways that we might not have considered. For example, let's say that when I ask my daughter to clean her room, I also tell her that I want to have less to do around the house on "cleaning day," a day when she'll be in school. Hearing my reasons, she explains that she's in the middle of a project that's spread all over her room and that she won't finish until after cleaning day. She then offers to clean her room two days later when she's finished with the project and also to help by cleaning one of the bathrooms before "cleaning day." Everybody wins! She gets to finish her project and I get the help I want.

I'm not saying that you always need to have reasons for your requests, only that it helps to share them if you do. Everyone has the right to ask for whatever he or she wants without any reason whatsoever, just because they want it. But sharing your reasons for making a request will increase the likelihood of getting your wishes fulfilled.

The best environment for successful requesting is cooperation, and the best method is open discussion and negotiation. People are more willing to honor requests when we're willing to also consider their needs. For example, when I request that my daughter clean her room, she's likely to say that she doesn't have enough time. If we have a cooperative relationship, she might ask me to help her save some time by driving her home from school and she can, in turn, honor my request. My willingness to help and her willingness to ask create a cooperative environment where we can work together to both get what we want. We are creating an environment that respects that our lives intertwine, learning in the process that the best environment for being together is one in which we feel committed to helping everyone get what they want.

Listening for intention and specificity

When others make requests without stating their reasons, it's important that we not only listen carefully to what they say, but also for the intentions behind their requests. We can easily uncover the intentions behind a request by asking, "What will that do for you?" This is better than asking why, which someone could hear as questioning their right to ask for what they want. Asking, "What will that do for you?" helps us to fulfill requests, rather than challenge them.

Unfortunately, people don't always state what they want explicitly enough to let us know exactly what they mean. Therefore, when a request is not perfectly clear to us, asking questions can clarify exactly what they want. When I request that my daughter clean her room, she might hear that as tidying up, but I might really want her to tidy up and vacuum. If she asked me what I meant, I could be more specific. In this instance, the difference may not be crucial, but some miscommunications can create more serious problems.

A stronger example is when I request that my wife do more to get along with my family. This is direct but not very specific. After agreeing to do more, with her background, she might think that I want her to not talk so much, when what I really want is for her to be more open with them by talking more. Not stating what I want explicitly makes our misunderstanding predictable. Eventually, I might end up feeling angry for having my request ignored while she feels hurt that I don't appreciate her efforts to honor my request.

The importance of voice tone

So far we've addressed what to say when making a request, but this is only part of a successful communication. *How* we speak greatly affects how others hear us. Our tone and inflection greatly influence how others hear our requests, often even more than the content. Using a tone and inflection that expresses respect and a mood of cooperation, one that's not whiny or critical, will influence others to honor your requests. Try playing with your voice tone and inflection, noticing how people respond. Discover what voice tones and inflections usually get the kind of responses that you want by conveying the true mood of your requests. You might feel surprised to discover how much your tone of voice and inflection affect the responses you get.

I strongly recommend mentally rehearsing requests before communicating them, giving special attention to what you're communicating with your voice. Are you communicating respect for the other person and a mood of cooperation, or impatience and a mood of criticism? You may even find it useful to use a tape recorder or get feedback from others. Learning to be intentional about how your requests sound will empower you to get the kinds of responses you really want.

How to Make a Request

1. Use a respectful, cooperative tone of voice.

2. Share the reasons for your request first.

3. Share what your request will do for you.

4. State that you want a change in behavior, not in the person.

5. Make your request a simple statement or question.

6. State your request in the positive.

7. Be as behaviorally specific as possible.

8. Be open to negotiation and discussion.

Transforming your relationships

Ideally, we can all replace our complaints with requests and thus create more open, cooperative relationships. However, when we've experienced a long history of complaining in a relationship, we can easily hear requests as complaints. Even during the beginning stages of a relationship, we can hear requests as complaints if we've brought a long history of being criticized into the relationship. Our challenge then is to create a new environment for our relationships, one in which we hear requests as requests and not complaints.

Transforming an environment filled with criticism and complaining into one filled with requests and mutual support is hard work. Significantly changing a relationship requires a lot of discussion and personal sharing. This should include not only what we want in the future but also how our past communication affected us.

When we change a relationship, we are in a sense recreating it, and in order to recreate a relationship we need to bring our attention into present time. As I stated earlier, bringing our attention into the present requires forgiving past mistakes by admitting what we've done and taking responsibility for learning from them. In order to change a complaint filled relationship into one managed with requests we must first take responsibility for past complaining, then forgive each other and finally commit ourselves to using requests in the future.

Getting help from others to identify past mistakes by listening to their account of how you've been, not as if it is the only truth, but with an openness and humility that respects their experience of what happened, will revive a suffering relationship. By remembering that you are the doer not the deed, you will be opening yourself to useful feedback, including the damage that you knowingly or unknowingly wrought in your relationships. This can prove to be a very painful process. But when you summon the courage to witness what you've done, take responsibility for your part in your relationships not working in the past and honestly commit yourself to changing how you communicate, you will create room for healing and the development of new, healthier relationships.

Unfortunately, even when we've purged all the demons from our past, we might not hear requests as something other than complaining. But there are ways to create an environment where we can feel honored enough to be able to hear requests as requests. This is through the free expression of our appreciation for each other.

Tool #3—Expressing Appreciation

Since David and Margaret's divorce, their 14 year-old daughter, Jennifer, has lived alternate weeks with each of them. Now seven years since their separation, David is remarried and has a two-year old son with his second wife, who is pregnant with their second child. Both David and Margaret agree that they communicate well as co-parents and they are committed to doing a good job raising Jennifer together. Jennifer has a good relationship with her step-mother, Sally, who treats her well and respects Jennifer's relationship with her mother. Jennifer loves her little brother and likes to baby-sit for him. Margaret acknowl-edges that Sally treats Jennifer well and supports David in his relationship with his new family. Clearly David and Margaret have done better with their divorce than they did with their marriage.

Jennifer is a good kid. She has nice friends, does well in school and has never been in any serious trouble. Yet recently, Jennifer has been wanting to spend less time with David. Like a typical 14-year-old, she doesn't talk much about her feelings, but she has told Margaret that she feels that her dad is always criticizing her, that he's never happy with anything she does. When Margaret talked to David about Jennifer's feelings, he said that lately Jennifer has been rude, surly and refuses to do anything that he asks her to do. He's told Jennifer that he finds her behavior unac-ceptable, but she just shrugs her shoulders at him and goes to her room. Thinking about the situation, Margaret recalls that one reason she and David broke up was that she felt unappreciated by him. She felt taken for granted, and he never seemed satisfied with what she did. She is hesitant to bring this up with David because, whenever she did during their marriage, they had awful arguments and David got defensive and angry with her. But Margaret has learned a few things since their divorce, so instead of talking to him directly, she decides to send David a letter acknowledging the ways that she thinks he's been a good father. David feels moved by the letter and calls Margaret to thank her. During the conversation, he asks her what she thinks he might do to improve his relationship with Jennifer. After patting herself on the back, Margaret talks to David about how insecure teenagers are and how much Jennifer needs to hear from him that he appreciates what she does.

Appreciation and acknowledgment are powerful tools. Margaret did a great job acknowledging David, creating a clear opening for communication. Because of the environment she had created, he could listen to what she had to say and even ask for help.

The key to creating relationships in which we hear requests for what they are is verbally expressing our appreciation and acknowledgment to each other. This includes both expressing our thanks for what others do and acknowledging their basic value and goodness. For example, I might appreciate my daughter by thanking her for helping me with the dishes or telling her how much I value how patient she is with her younger sister. Acknowledgment means expressing how we truly feel about others, telling them how important they are to us in our lives. I can acknowledge my daughter by telling her how lucky I feel to have her in my life.

When we feel appreciated and acknowledged by others, we can hear their requests to us as merely requests and not fall back into old patterns of feeling criticized. Feeling appreciated, we experience requests as possible ways to improve our relationships, not statements about our personal shortcomings. When David felt appreciated by Margaret, he became open to her suggestions for how to improve his relationship with Jennifer.

When my wife asks me to spend more time with our daughters, if I feel appreciated by her for what I'm already doing well, I hear this as a request, not a criticism. Fortunately, my wife is a master at expressing appreciation and often tells me what a good father I am. Already feeling appreciated by her, I can hear her request as a suggestion about how to improve my relationship with my daughters.

On the other hand, when I feel unappreciated, I might hear her request as a masked complaint that I'm not doing enough with my daughters, as criticism of my fathering. That my wife appreciates my fathering, however, is not enough to insure that I hear her request as a request. For me to know that she appreciates what I'm doing she must express it to me.

Creating an environment of appreciation

What goes around comes around, so the best way to encourage others to express their appreciation to you is to freely express your appreciation to them. People who feel appreciated will feel better about themselves, and people who feel good about themselves will more easily recognize another's contribution and express their appreciation for it. When my wife and I express our appreciation for our oldest daughter, she's more able to express appreciation for her younger sister. Margaret expressing her appreciation to David will make it easier for him to express his appreciation to Jennifer. Expressing appreciation surrounds us with people who feel honored and valued and who will recognize and appreciate our contribution in turn.

Even though appreciating others seems to be natural and easy, the free expression of appreciation is rare. You can get striking evidence for this by going to a funeral and listening to the survivors. You'll hear people say that they wished that they had told the deceased how much he or she meant to them and how they loved and appreciated the departed. We need to express our appreciation for those we love before it's too late.

Appreciating and not expressing it

Most of us really do appreciate what others do for us, but we often fail to express our appreciation as much as we feel it. Before I discovered the power of expressing appreciation, my feelings of appreciation for others went largely unexpressed. I can remember a relationship in college in which my girlfriend and I both felt taken for granted. This was our way of saying that we didn't feel appreciated. I can look back on it now and recognize that I did appreciate her, but I just didn't express it to her. After a while, as our feelings of being unappreciated accumulated, we grew apart and our relationship ended.

When we don't feel appreciated, we feel hurt and try to distance ourselves from our hurt by distancing ourselves from those we love. Distancing ourselves from each other, we become less able to feel appreciative because we're less likely to notice those things they do that deserve appreciation. Feeling more and more unappreciated, we drift farther and farther apart. Because Jennifer felt that her father didn't appreciate her, she isolated herself and became less inclined to appreciate what her younger brother did.

Even when we feel appreciation for what others do, we often don't express it. For example, David surely appreciates his daughter. That's why he wants to spend time with her, but he consistently failed to tell her how he felt. Where did we learn to hold back expressing our appreciation? What do we believe that holds us back from expressing the appreciation we feel? Discovering the answers to these questions can help us develop new beliefs and attitudes that will support us in learning to express our appreciation for those we love. But before we can explore what beliefs inhibit our expression of appreciation, we first must understand how we all learn what we believe to be true.

How we learn

There are two major mechanisms for learning how to behave, think and feel as human beings. The first is through modeling those around us. As children we all observe how those around us behave. As soon as we can, we begin imitating our relatives and friends. This is modeling. All cultures and families have their own unique ways of doing things. A simple cultural example is Europeans learning to eat food with forks and spoons, while Asians learn to eat with chopsticks. A more significant cultural difference is the respect and care that Asians show for their elders compared to our own Western attitudes and behaviors that lean more towards separation and tolerance. In the same way, individual families have their own ways of doing things. For example, some families encourage their children to spontaneously express their thoughts and feelings, while other families want children to "only speak when they're spoken to."

We learn how to be human by observing those around us. My father showed me how to be a man in a way that is both somewhat different from and somewhat similar to how other boys learned to be men from their fathers. I learned a lot about providing for my family and being reliable and faithful to my wife from him. However, I also learned that men don't talk about their feelings.

Fortunately, we're not doomed to be exactly like our parents. Because each of us has inherent tendencies, we're selective about what we model. Some things we copy directly, some we change slightly, some we do the opposite and some we change completely. We also continue to model others as we grow; but even when I do something differently from my father, I probably used other people as models for my new behavior. I learned to talk about my feelings from men I met in college who modeled this for me.

The second way we learn is by responding to the things that happen to us. This includes not only the events that occur but also what others communicate to us both verbally and nonverbally. The young boy whose parents beat him when he breaks a cup might learn to hide his mistakes or even become afraid to do things. The young girl who feels ignored when she expresses her opinion learns to keep her opinion to herself.

We also respond to what is absent in our families. The young singer whose parents never come to a performance might decide to stop singing. The child whose parents are going through divorce and never talk to him about why dad moved out might decide that his dad doesn't love him anymore.

Many factors influence our response to what happens to us. How we think and feel about our early experiences, our environment and our personal state of being all shape our response to early experiences. Consequently, different people can have different responses to the same experience. Also, context affects someone's response to an event. For example, when I get impatient with my daughter and criticize what she's doing, if I normally treat her with respect and support, she might experience my criticism as "dad's in a bad mood" and not react very strongly to it. It probably wouldn't have much impact on how she feels about herself. However, if criticism was my primary way of relating to her, my treatment could deeply affect how she feels about herself. She might develop feelings of worthlessness and later develop a strong need to prove herself to men who are "never satisfied anyway." Also, each of my daughters might react differently because they have different strengths and temperaments. This is how people who come from very similar backgrounds can be very different in how they experience and consequently respond to their upbringing.

Generalization: How we apply what we learn

After learning how to "be" — that is, how to think, feel and behave — through modeling and in response to our experience, we apply what we've learned to our present lives through a process called generalization. Generalization helps me to know that I can sit in a chair I've never seen before because it's enough like other chairs that I've sat in before.

Generalization is necessary to function in the world. It saves us from having to spend precious time learning about every detail of every new situation. Without generalization, every time I got in a car I would have to learn how to drive all over again. This is how generalization serves us. If a situation is similar to past experiences, we generalize our past learnings from these past experiences so that we don't have to relearn everything.

Our past experiences strongly shape how we think, feel, and act. For example, the young girl, whose parents chastise her whenever she expresses herself, learns to keep quiet at home in order to avoid her parents' criticism. Later, as a new wife, she is likely to find it difficult to express her opinions to her husband. She has generalized the emotional survival technique of her childhood, treating her husband as if he is like her parents.

Because this process of generalization is neutral, we generalize both positive and negative experiences. Unfortunately, we often generalize something we've learned to a new situation where the learning doesn't really apply. The young woman who keeps her opinion to herself in her marriage might be living with a man who would not only honor, but also greatly value, knowing what she thinks. If so, she's acting out her past learning in ways which could prove to be detrimental to the future of her marriage. After years of not knowing what his wife thinks, her husband could easily grow tired of feeling emotionally isolated from her.

To summarize, we learn how to be by modeling how others act, think and feel, and through our adaptive response to our experiences. We then apply these learnings to our lives by generalizing what we've learned to similar situations. Let's consider now what we've learned and generalized about expressing and not expressing our appreciation for each other.

Appreciation in the past

Most of us come from families where there was little direct expression of appreciation. Consequently, because we've rarely witnessed family members expressing appreciation for each other, we have few models for expressing appreciation. Without models we have little reference for knowing how to express appreciation. Most of our parents and elders have demonstrated almost no direct expression of appreciation and were awkward and uncomfortable when they did. We can guess that Jennifer's father, David, had few models for expressing appreciation. Those who come from families who expressed appreciation openly are fortunate exceptions to the general experience that most of us have had in our culture.

This lack of expression is consistent with our cultural tradition of rarely communicating things of a personal nature. Few of us come from families that communicated directly and fully about personal matters. We talk about the weather or what happened, rarely about how we feel about each other.

We all have some hurtful memories of not having been sufficiently appreciated for something we did well, situations in which we desired and deserved to be appreciated but were not. I'm sure that each of you can think of a personal memory like this. Maybe you weren't acknowledged for working hard at school, or taking care of a sibling or trying out for a sports team. Whatever the case, we all seem to have some negative experience of not being appreciated when we should have been.

Appreciation in the present

Lacking good models can make expressing appreciation very uncomfortable. Not knowing exactly how to do it, we can feel awkward and self-conscious about it. These feelings alone are enough to keep most of us from expressing our appreciation, but there is an even stronger obstacle.

Combining few experiences of being appreciated with enough experiences of not being appreciated, when we deserved to be, can teach us to associate appreciation with feeling bad. Consequently, times that call for us to appreciate someone else only serve as reminders of our own hurt feelings from not having been appreciated ourselves. It's hard to express our feelings of appreciation for others when we associate appreciating others with feeling bad. Even witnessing others being appreciated can make us envious and stimulate these bad feelings from not having been appreciated ourselves. The young man whose parents fail to praise him for getting good grades is not likely to praise his younger sister for her good grades.

Not appreciating others and feeling envious when others are appreciated are both unconscious responses. We usually aren't consciously aware that our present responses are rooted in past experiences of not having been sufficiently appreciated ourselves. Instead of consciously deciding to not express our appreciation, we simply don't notice what begs appreciation, or forget to do it. David probably had no idea that Jennifer felt unappreciated by him until Margaret told him. If asked, most of us would agree that others deserve appreciation, however, this is a lot like recognizing that we need to exercise and eat well. Usually our conscious beliefs have little effect on our actual behavior. Our unconscious feelings and associations determine what we actually do.

Two beliefs that support not expressing appreciation

Over the years, we've developed some commonly held beliefs that support not expressing our appreciation. These beliefs serve us by helping to rationalize our behavior. So in order to change our behavior, we must first challenge these beliefs.

The first belief that seriously inhibits our free expression of appreciation is that **there is a limit to things**. This attitude of limitation affects our behavior in many areas of our lives, including money, good fortune and the free expression of love and compassion. We behave as if there's not enough to go around, that if we are too freely giving in the present, supplies will run out. We don't express appreciation for others because we fear that when it's time for others to appreciate us, the appreciation account will be empty. This attitude makes no sense; but it's easy for those of us who haven't been appreciated enough to mistakenly conclude that there's not enough to go around. Believing that there's a limit to things is a deeply hidden, pervasive cultural attitude.

The second belief that inhibits our free expression of appreciation is that **praising people too much makes them lazy and unmotivated**. Underlying this belief is another one that alleges that we are most motivated to do more when we feel bad about what we have done. We believe that if we praise people too much, they'll fail to recognize their shortcomings and lose their motivation to improve. With this belief, we actually think that we help others avoid being lazy by not expressing our appreciation directly to them.

Beliefs that empower us to express our appreciation

If limitations exist at all in this world, they occur only in the physical and material realms of existence. We can have too little food to feed everyone or not enough rain forests to replenish the ozone layer. However, there is absolutely no limit to non-material things like love, caring, support, appreciation and forgiveness. These are not material things, and we limit them only by treating them as scarce resources and feeling too afraid and inhibited to express ourselves freely to each other. An environment of free expression of love and appreciation will only lead to more expression of love and appreciation. Feeling loved and appreciated empowers us to express our feelings of love and appreciation to others. When Jennifer feels appreciated by her father she'll feel more inclined to appreciate her brother.

Rather than making us lazy and unmotivated, praise helps us feel that what we're doing makes a difference. Praise serves as a reward that motivates us to continue the behavior that attracted the praise. Instead of preventing us from addressing our shortcomings, feeling appreciated creates an environment where we feel safe enough to examine them; and we know that others will notice and acknowledge our accomplishments as we improve.

Creating an environment that supports appreciation requires that we believe that there's enough appreciation to go around and that praise helps us stay motivated to improve our shortcomings. These beliefs will support us in healing our hurt feelings from not having been appreciated in the past and help us create new positive associations for our expression of appreciation.

Beliefs

Beliefs that support not expressing appreciation:

1. There is a limit to things.
2. Praising people will make them lazy and unmotivated.

Beliefs that support expressing appreciation:

1. There is more than enough to go around.
2. Praise motivates people.

How we can change

To freely express our appreciation for others we need to change our relationship to past negative experiences of not having been appreciated when we deserved to be. If we can successfully free ourselves from our past we will be able to express the appreciation that we now feel. We can then replace our old automatic responses with new behaviors that more closely reflect our present attitudes and feelings.

Freeing himself from his past of not having been appreciated himself will make it easier for David to express his appreciation to Jennifer. The question is how do we free ourselves from these negative associations.

Getting free of past experiences requires fully processing these experiences, both mentally and emotionally. In our culture, we most often fail to process experiences by not recognizing and resolving our feelings or emotions from these experiences. For example, my father almost never praised me for my accomplishments. I was a good student, bringing home A's. His response was to kid me, wondering aloud why I hadn't gotten an A+. This hurt me; but I didn't express my hurt at the time because I'd learned that it was unmanly to feel hurt by something so unimportant and trivial. After all, he was only kidding. But it wasn't the kidding that hurt most, it was the praise that went unexpressed. Eventually, I learned to bury my feelings so efficiently that I became unaware of feeling hurt. Only later as an adult did I recover my awareness of how hurt I felt. I realized that underneath the envy I felt whenever anyone besides myself received praise was a great deal of hurt. In time, uncovering and resolving these hurt feelings freed me to be more gracious when others do things that deserve appreciation.

Fully processing our past experiences must include identifying and resolving any emotions that we felt during these experiences. This is something we often neglect when trying to change. We often try to think ourselves into changing without this important step of resolving our emotions, emotions that have largely shaped our present dysfunctional behavior. But identifying and resolving our emotions requires that we have a clear understanding of the nature of emotions, including understanding how our traditional methods for dealing with our emotions keep us from moving through them. This discussion of the nature of emotions and how to resolve them is the subject of the next chapter. You may find it most useful to read that chapter now, before completing the rest of this chapter.

Freeing ourselves to express our appreciation

The first step in freeing ourselves to fully express our appreciation is to identify our past experiences of not feeling sufficiently appreciated. Next we need to recover how we felt at the time, and to accept and fully express these feelings. After acknowledging and accepting these feelings, without becoming righteous about them, we can forgive those who failed to express the appreciation we deserved. When David realizes the source of his stinginess about expressing his appreciation and releases his feelings from these experiences, he'll become freer to express his appreciation.

When I figured out that my feeling bad when others receive appreciation comes from my past experiences with my dad, I realized how deeply hurt I felt. With the help of people who love and support me I was able to cry and talk about how I felt unappreciated by my father. I could then forgive him and recognize that his lack of expression was rooted in his past experience and not a reflection of how he really felt about me.

A great way to begin healing our present relationships is to share this process with each other, helping us all be more receptive to any positive changes we make. Though sharing what we're learning and our feelings does not excuse our past behavior, it does create new intimacy.

Witnessing each other's transformation helps us to understand these changes that we're all making and accept them as real and genuine. Ultimately, we will begin to express the appreciation we've felt but left unexpressed and create supportive, loving relationships.

Completing past experiences by acknowledging and expressing our feelings from them frees us to celebrate our love for each other through our expressed appreciation and acknowledgment. Understanding that there's no limit to the expression of love in the form of appreciation, and trusting that our expressed appreciation is the best guarantee of thoughtful and positive behavior, we can express our appreciation without restraint or inhibition. In this environment of free expression of appreciation and acknowledgment, requests become a way to better relationships. Feeling appreciated, it's easier to understand another's request as valuable information that we can use to build healthier relationships.

Tool #4—Moving Through Emotions

In the last section, I suggested that freeing ourselves from a past of not feeling appreciated requires fully processing our experience. An essential part of processing and eventually evolving beyond these or any limiting experience is identifying and resolving our emotions from these experiences. In this section, I offer you tools for gaining a new understanding of your emotions that you can use to resolve your past experience. You can then use these tools to more easily respond to your present experience without unwanted negative influence from the past.

Throughout her life, Carla, 28, has had poor relationships with men. She describes her childhood relationship with her father as alright, but distant. Whenever she visits her parents, which is usually about twice a year, she loves to see her sister and mother, but she and her father don't have much to say to each other. When Carla entered therapy to work on her problems with men, she told her therapist about her tendency to pick men who were controlling and emotionally distant. Then after building up enough hurt feelings from how they treat her, she withdraws from them. Subsequently, any love they once felt for each other fades and the relationship ends.

As she began to explore these experiences with her therapist she realized that how she felt with her lovers was the same way that she had always felt with her father. She began to remember that her father had been very critical of her, seemingly never satisfied with anything she did. He was also emotionally distant and controlling, constantly telling her what she should and shouldn't do in her life. How she dealt with this as a child was to withdraw from him without expressing how she felt, learning to repress her emotions very early in life.

This insight made a powerful impact on Carla. It helped her recover some very strong emotions from these early experiences. With encouragement from her therapist, she was able to release many of these emotions, expressing her hurt through tears and her anger verbally and physically in ways that didn't hurt anyone. She and her therapist agreed that she was right to feel hurt and angry with her father for how he treated her. Unfortunately, her therapist also encouraged her to call her father and confront him. As could be expected, he reacted poorly. He couldn't understand why she felt so hurt and angry, telling her that he had always loved her and couldn't remember doing anything that deserved such a strong, negative reaction. This made her even angrier and she hung up on him. Two years later, she was still angry with him. She hadn't been home to visit since their phone call, and even though she's been in touch with her mother and sister over the phone, she feels that coming home would be too hard on her. Everyone is suffering. Carla feels awful about avoiding her family, but she doesn't know what to do. She feels that if she goes back to how things were, she would be saying that she's okay with how her father treated her; but by staying away she feels isolated and cut off from them. By the way, she still hasn't had a good relationship with a man.

Carla came to me for help because a friend told her that I was good at helping people create real changes in their lives. She told me a longer version of her story, saying that she feels stuck with her present therapist. I assured her that I could help, suggesting that even though her therapy was helpful, it had fallen short. Her therapist, with good intentions, had helped her to recover her repressed emotions but had failed to take her through the next step to health and emotional well-being. I knew that gaining a better understanding of forgiving and the nature of her emotions would help Carla get where she wanted to go, having a healthy relationship with a man and a new, healthier relationship with her family.

In this chapter, I will describe how our old attitudes and beliefs about emotions have prevented us from successfully moving through them. I will then offer you four principles for a new understanding of emotions that will empower you to smoothly move through all your emotions as they arise.

Our traditional attitudes about emotions

Feeling emotions is one form of human expression. The others are doing and thinking. That's it, that's all there is. All our human expression is some combination of doing, thinking and feeling. We are always doing something, thinking something and feeling something. All are equally important, but we seem to understand our feelings the least.

For various reasons we've learned to feel uncomfortable with our emotions. Maybe our parents became uncomfortable or even angry when we cried as small children, or maybe we were questioned and challenged about whether we had good enough reasons to feel what we were feeling. Whatever our personal history with emotions, as a culture we seem to lack a useful and healthy attitude about them. We are frequently unaware of what we are feeling, and even when we do become aware of an emotion, we don't know quite what to do with it. We avoid negative feelings, such as hurt and sadness because we think that feeling bad means something is wrong. Overly committed to feeling good all the time, we deny ourselves awareness of our full range of emotional experience, operating under the illusion that a happy life means never feeling bad.

Unfortunately, we have failed to recognize that denying ourselves the experience of uncomfortable emotions closes us off to all our emotions. Avoiding feeling bad because we want to feel good denies the paradox that being open to all our feelings, even those that feel bad, determines our capacity to feel good. We can enjoy a rich, happy life only when we welcome all of our emotions, experiencing them fully and moving through them freely and gracefully. But in order to experience our emotions without resistance and move through them with grace we need a new understanding of emotions.

How we have misunderstood the nature of our emotions

Traditionally, we've dealt with our emotions by questioning their validity. We have operated as if some emotions were valid and some were not, with valid emotions being those we had good enough reasons to feel. If I felt angry, I needed a good enough reason to justify my anger. If I felt sad, something sufficiently tragic must have happened to justify my sadness. Those emotions we could justify were okay to feel, but those we could not justify were not. We could feel what we felt only when we had good enough reasons.

I can remember childhood experiences of crying because my feelings were hurt and well-meaning adults trying to make me feel better by telling me there was nothing for me to cry about. Being a quick learner, I began to question the validity of my feelings, and years later I heard myself saying the same thing to my young daughter. She was crying about not getting a Barbie that she had wanted at the store, a disappointment that seemed small and insignificant to me, when I heard myself telling her, "that's nothing to be upset about." Fortunately, my wife saved me from passing on this tradition to my daughter by pointing out that if there were nothing to be upset about, she wouldn't be upset!

Questioning their validity makes emotions subordinate to our thinking, the realm of reason and rationale. Consequently, whenever we feel emotions we try to justify them by finding good reasons to validate what we feel, thus experiencing our emotions as either right or wrong. As a boy I needed a good enough reason, something important, to justify my crying. When I could find justifiable reasons to feel upset, I was "right" to feel hurt. Without justifiable reasons, I was "wrong" to feel upset.

In a world where feelings must be justified, children need to find reasons for their feelings, reasons that their parents and peers find acceptable. In the example above, my daughter could only feel bad if she had reasons that I thought were good enough to justify her feeling bad. Even after becoming adults, we can find ourselves still trying to find reasons that justify how we feel to our parents.

How our misunderstanding shapes our response to our emotions

When we must justify our feelings, we learn to respond to our emotions by either becoming righteous about them or repressing them. If we can justify our emotions with good enough reasons, we become righteous about what we feel.

We are literally "right" to feel what we feel. If I forget our anniversary, my wife is "right" to feel hurt and angry with me. When my father died I was "right" to feel sad. When our feelings are either "right" or "wrong," the only emotions we allow ourselves to feel are "righteous" ones.

On the other hand, when we can't sufficiently justify an emotion we repress it. Feeling emotions that we can't justify creates a conflict between what we feel and what we're allowed to feel. In the example above, if my daughter had listened to me, she would have experienced conflict between feeling upset and feeling "wrong" to feel upset. The natural human response to this type of conflict is to repress the original upset feelings, seemingly resolving the conflict.

Because we grow up feeling lots of emotions that we can't sufficiently justify, repressing our emotions can eventually become a habit. Like any habit, we learn to do it without consciously knowing that we are. If we feel an emotion that we can't justify, we automatically repress it before we're even consciously aware of it. We can learn to seemingly move through life without much feeling or emotion at all.

In most families, we learn to repress those feelings we can't justify and express those we can; but when families react negatively to any strong expression of emotion, we can learn to repress all of our feelings. Some families have unspoken taboos about particular emotions. Observing how our families respond to the situations that occur in life, we can learn that it's not okay to feel certain emotions at all. The small boy who gets ridiculed when he expresses his fear might learn to habitually repress his fear. The young woman who lives in a family with no acknowledgment or expression of angry feelings learns that it's never all right to feel angry. In the extreme it's possible to learn that all emotions are a sign of weakness and eventually learn to repress all or most of our emotions, becoming adults who either feel nothing or feel only those rare righteous feelings we can sufficiently justify.

The problem with repression and righteousness

Even though repressing emotions is very different from feeling righteous about them, both these responses keep us stuck in our feelings. Repressing a feeling doesn't get rid of it because, when we repress a feeling, we merely become unconscious to what we're feeling. Repressed feelings don't change; they just become more deeply buried under more repression as the years go by, and no matter how deeply we bury them, they still affect us. Feelings that we first felt decades ago can still run our lives. Many times in my marriage, I've seriously overreacted to my wife, responding in a way that was way out of proportion to what she'd done. I can remember getting very angry whenever she disagreed with something that was important to me. Eventually, after closer self-examination I discovered that I had repressed many hurt feelings from past experiences when I felt that my parents and teachers were not honoring my opinions. These repressed emotions never went away and eventually dictated my response to my wife. When she expressed any disagreement with me, I felt the old hurt that I had repressed and got angry with her. Fortunately, I now understand that she was just expressing her opinion, not telling me that I didn't have the right to mine.

I suspect that you can identify situations in which you overreacted to what was happening. If so, you can conclude that some old repressed emotions were being triggered and this led to your disproportionate response. Ultimately, the more you have repressed your emotions, the more you react to present situations in old habitual ways.

When we *can* find sufficient reasons for our feelings, we also get stuck in them. When we use reasons to validate our feelings, any possibility of moving past our feelings requires admitting that our reasons were invalid in the first place, that our feelings were "wrong." However, since like most people we would rather be right than happy, we're reluctant to admit that we were wrong, and so we cling to our righteous feelings.

In the course of therapy, many of my clients uncover repressed emotions. An important part of my job is keeping them from becoming righteous about these recovered emotions. The young woman who uncovers feelings from being verbally abused as a child by her mother can easily justify feeling hurt and angry. However, if I collude with her in justifying her feelings, she will stay stuck in them, making it difficult to heal her wounds from these experiences and preventing her from moving on to forgiveness and a new understanding of her relationship with her mother. If I help her continue to justify her hurt and anger, she will stay stuck in these feelings because she's "right" to feel what she feels. Instead, if I help her to validate her feelings, without needing to justify them, she can move through them, get on with her life and maybe even create the kind of relationship she would like to have with her mother now.

As an example, let's consider how repression and righteousness shape our experience of anger. When we repress anger because we can't justify it, we don't even know that we still feel angry. But our anger is still there and usually comes out by overreacting to something else. We might emotionally explode over some insignificant event or get angry with our kids over something really trivial when we are really feeling angry with our boss. In the extreme, repressed anger leads to passive-aggressive behavior. An example of passive-aggressive behavior is when I just happen to drop and break my wife's favorite mug after insisting I'm not angry that she forgot about my birthday. When we feel angry and repress our anger it always comes out in some way.

When I'm angry and feel "right" to be angry, I stay angry. Years later the event can come up in conversation and I'll still feel angry about it. We've all known people who have loved each other but let their anger and hurt feelings get between them. Being "right" to feel angry, no one wants to admit that they were wrong, so they hang onto their anger. Years can go by without letting their anger go. I have a childhood memory of two of my father's cousins, brothers, not speaking to each other for ten years because of a relatively minor disagreement. They were both too busy feeling "right" and avoiding being "wrong" to realize what it was costing them.

When we repress our feelings they continue to influence us unconsciously, seriously affecting our reactions and behavior. When we're righteous about our feelings, we hang onto them to avoid being wrong.

Three Ways to Handle Our Emotions:

a feelings flow chart

Something Happens ⇨ Internal Process

↙

Feelings/ Emotions

↙   ↘

My feelings are not   My feelings are
valid in and   valid in and
of themselves   of themselves

⇓   ⇓

Attempt to   Feel feelings/express
justify feelings   feelings appropriately

⇓   ↘   ⇓

Can justify   Cannot justify   Feelings pass

⇓   ⇓

Righteous   Repressed
feelings   feelings

⇓   ⇓

Hang onto   Hang onto
feelings to avoid   feelings
being wrong   unconsciously

↘   ↙

Feelings run my life

Four principles for a new understanding of emotions

The first, and most important, principle of a new understanding of emotions is that **all emotions are valid in and of themselves**. All our emotions are valid merely because we feel them. We don't need to justify our feelings with reasons because they are always already valid. When all our feelings are valid we remove emotions from the realm of "right" or "wrong." We no longer need to justify what we feel. Therefore, we never need to repress our "wrong" feelings because there's no such thing as a "wrong" feeling. We are never righteous about our feelings because feelings are neither "right" nor "wrong." We just feel what we feel. The young woman who uncovered her repressed anger at her mother can understand that her angry feelings are valid just because she feels them. She doesn't need to justify them, nor does she need to be righteous about them. Free to feel what she feels just because she feels it, she can eventually let go of her anger because moving past her anger doesn't invalidate having felt angry before.

The second principle is that **all feelings are subjective and personal**. It doesn't matter whether someone else would feel the same way in the same situation or even that we might react differently at different times to two seemingly identical occurrences. We feel what we feel when we feel it, and that's it. My daughter might feel upset about something that would not upset me, but that doesn't invalidate either her or my feelings. Just as one person's opinion is as valid as another person's opinion, because they are only opinions, everyone's feelings are valid.

In the same way, we can have different responses to the same experience. On a day that I feel strong, I might react to someone's lack of consideration with understanding. On a day that I feel tired and unresourceful, I might react with hurt feelings to virtually the same experience. Our reactions to what happens to us can change from day to day and moment to moment depending on our state of being. That we can feel differently from each other, and even from ourselves at times, is the beauty of living in a world of variety and differing experience.

The third principle is that **present feelings and future feelings require different responses**. Present feelings exist, while future feelings have not yet happened. We can change our behavior and affect how we will feel in the future, but we can't change present feelings — we can only move through them. In fact, moving through present feelings can help us change future emotional reactions. Let me use an example to clarify this principle.

Let's say that I feel envious when I read that someone else has published a successful book about relationships. For a long time I've realized that envy is an emotion that doesn't serve me in any way. It only reinforces the belief that there's not enough to go around. Since I want to live in a world of abundance, it would better serve me to feel supportive of someone else publishing a successful book, understanding that this is a good indication that there's a healthy audience for what I have to offer in my own writing. However, all this understanding doesn't change what I've already felt. My envious feelings exist, and I need to acknowledge them and perhaps express them. Making my present feelings neither right nor wrong, I can move through them. Once they subside, I can think about how I might like to feel in the future in similar situations and figure out how to do that. I may need to recover old memories of feeling hurt for not being acknowledged, resolve these old hurt feelings and free myself from them. If I do this, perhaps the next time I read about someone's successful book on relationships, I'll feel happy for them. If I do, great. If I still feel envious, then I need to acknowledge and express these feelings and, if I choose to, do some more work that might change my reaction in the future.

When we feel feelings that don't serve us, being okay with our present feelings empowers us to change our future response. Changes we make now can only affect the future. I'm not saying that change needs to be slow. After all, five seconds from now is the future, as well as five years from now. I am pointing out that changing our emotional reactions is paradoxical. Accepting and expressing what we've already felt helps us change, while resisting what we've already felt keeps us stuck in old patterns.

The fourth, and last, principle is that **feeling an emotion and expressing it are two different things**. All feelings are valid, but all expressions of emotions are not. Many factors determine the appropriateness of our expression, including family values, culture and circumstance. A woman's angry feelings toward her father for past abuse are valid because she feels them. However, the validity of her anger is distinct from her decision to confront her father. Her anger is valid whether she confronts her father or not. Her decision to confront her father needs to depend more on what kind of relationship she wants to have with him now and whether he seems to have changed over the years. But the way she chooses to express her anger doesn't change the validity of her feelings.

Four Principles for a New Understanding of Emotions

1. All feelings are valid in and of themselves.
2. All feelings are subjective.
3. Present feelings and future feelings require different treatment.
4. Feeling an emotion and expressing it are two different things.

Some considerations of the four principles

When all feelings are valid in and of themselves, we never need to question a feeling. If I feel angry with my wife, I can choose to tell her what I feel. When she hears me, and I feel heard, I can move past feeling angry because I don't need to stay angry to justify my feeling. Whether I want to make a request of her or she wants to change something in her behavior in response to my feelings is another issue.

When all feelings are valid in and of themselves, we accept that feeling emotions is a normal part of human experience, and we never need to repress emotions. We realize that people have different natures and that some will be more emotional than others. Being strong means that we are able to act because of or in spite of what we feel, not that we don't feel.

Since feelings are subjective, there are no rules about what to feel and how long to feel it. But we do need to live with how our expression affects others. Moping around the house for days because my basketball team lost a game can make it hard for others to live with me. When we get stuck in an emotion for a while, we may need to consider whether we are righteously justifying our feelings. If we're being righteous, our feelings aren't likely to pass regardless of how much we express them.

Dealing with feelings is more of an art than a science. Feelings, like all experiences, are personal and subjective. Therefore, these principles can serve only as guidelines, providing a structure for the art of living while we fully experience all our emotions. These principles can serve us in the same way that understanding the nature of all the different paints and brushes helps a painter in his art. However, the painter still has to decide what to paint. In the same way, we still have to decide how to respond to and express our emotions.

How the new understanding of emotions makes life easier

When we hold our emotions as valid in and of themselves, we can move through them with ease and grace. We freely experience our feelings without attaching ourselves to them. We understand that if we don't resist our feelings, by repressing them or hanging on to them righteously, they will pass. The more we experience this natural flow of emotions, the more we trust that our feelings will pass, and the more we allow ourselves to be aware of what we feel.

When my daughter was very young, she seemed to favor her mother over me. When she felt upset, she would want her mama, not her daddy. I felt hurt. Repressing or justifying my hurt feelings would have guaranteed that I got stuck in these feelings. Instead I was able to share my feelings with my wife, who was very understanding and compassionate. Eventually, when she thought I was ready to hear it, she helped me understand that our daughter's behavior wasn't personal, but a function of both her age and the fact that my wife spent more time with her. Along with validating my feelings, this realization helped me get past my hurt feelings. The next time my daughter "rejected" me for my wife I didn't feel hurt. As my wife had predicted, in time my daughter's response to me evolved and now we are very close. Sometimes she'll even come to me for comfort when she and my wife are in conflict. If I hadn't moved through my hurt feelings, either by repressing them or holding onto them righteously, I could have easily distanced myself from my daughter to avoid being hurt again. This would have created an even more serious problem when my daughter became ready to bring me closer to her — I wouldn't have been there. Years later, we would have recalled that we loved each other but were never close.

Allowing ourselves to have our feelings and move through them helps us return to what we really want in our relationships without a lot of old emotional garbage getting in the way. When we're aware of what we feel, we avoid overreacting and displacing our feelings. We no longer come home and dump our feelings from work on our friends and family. Learning to be more aware of where our feelings come from, we can use our relationships to help us move through them. Our relationships can become like an oasis, a place of respite and peace, instead of a dumping ground. We can express our feelings and let them pass so that we can fully experience the pleasure of being together.

As we learn to let our emotions flow we create a space for deeper emotional experiences. The more we experience that our bad feelings pass, the less we hang onto them. Expressing our feelings can even lead to new understandings that will enable us to no longer react with hurt and anger to what others do. When I told my wife how hurt I felt from my daughter's reaction to me, she helped me get a new understanding of the situation that empowered me to react differently after that.

Ultimately, our awareness of what we feel will free us from being victims of our old reactive emotions. The more we become aware of and accept what we feel, the more we can develop understandings that can help us be less emotionally reactive. As we feel bad less and less of the time, we become more available to feeling more profound non-reactive emotions like love, peace and joy. These feelings come through the same channel as our reactive emotions. But, it's important to remember that we paradoxically create room for our non-reactive emotions to flow by accepting our reactive emotions when we feel them.

A useful way to think about our feelings is to imagine that we are channels, like the channel of a river, and that our emotions are the waters that flow through us. If we allow the waters to flow freely, all waters that flow through us will pass, creating space for more water to flow. And as we allow these waters to pass, they clear the way for the waters that follow, and so on, and so on. What allows the waters (our emotions) to flow is our acceptance, validation and expression. Repression and righteousness are obstructions that block the flow, causing the flow to slow down and even stop. Repressed feelings are like rocks that lie under the surface, creating blockages that we fail to see. Righteous feelings are rocks that we can see, creating blockage on the surface, but that we refuse to clear away because we feel so enamored with them. When we clear away the rocks that are our repressed and righteous feelings, the waters can flow freely and clearly.

Expressing our emotions

We must acknowledge and validate our emotions in order to have a healthy emotional life. Whether and how to express our emotions is a separate decision. There are, however, some distinct advantages to expressing emotions. Expressing our emotions will invite validation from others and help us become more comfortable with our emotions. By sharing her emotions with me, the verbally abused young woman was able to become more comfortable with her hurt and anger. Expressing our emotions also helps us move through them and ensures that we're not repressing our emotions. Without expressing my feelings to my wife, I could have easily convinced myself that I was all right with how my daughter was responding to me. Then I would have been repressing my feelings when I thought I was really transcending them.

While generally supporting our expression of emotions, we need to understand that some forms of expression are more acceptable and constructive than others. Telling someone that I feel angry with him or her is quite different from being verbally or physically abusive. The best guideline for expressing emotions is to do no harm, to express our emotions in a way that respects others. We are human, however, and sometimes we might express our feelings in ways that are harmful to others. Even this is an opportunity to admit what we've done, apologize, forgive ourselves and learn from our experience.

Some of us hesitate to express our feelings because we fear letting our emotions determine our behavior. We falsely think that our fear of doing something, like making a presentation, will stop us. However, exactly the opposite is true. When we repress our feelings, they shape our behavior. Our repressed feelings come out unconsciously and automatically in what we say and do. This is how others can sometimes think we're angry or annoyed when we feel nothing consciously.

On the other hand, when we're aware of our feelings, we get to choose our behavior in spite of what we feel. We can be afraid to make an important presentation and still go ahead with it. We can decide to not do something because we think it might not be a good idea, rather than letting our fear stop us.

What we feel and what we do become independent of each other only when we're aware of what we're feeling. For example, courage comes from being aware of our fear and acting in spite of it. Those who claim to feel no fear when there's very real danger can't be fully trusted because we never know when their fear will surface and their "courage" will fail them.

When expressing our feelings, timing is very important. During my wife's birthday party might not be the best time to tell her that I feel angry about something she did the day before. It's fine, and sometimes preferable, to put off sharing our feelings to a better time and place, as long as we remember to eventually deal with our feelings.

That others are sometimes upset when we express our emotions doesn't necessarily mean that we've failed to express ourselves in a respectful way. It is important that we check out whether we have been thoughtful and respectful in our expression, but even the most thoughtful expression can trigger an emotional response from someone else. A friend of mine told her boyfriend that she felt upset about how distant he was being. His reaction was to feel hurt and angry. Knowing him, I can guess that he felt hurt because it's not okay for him to be imperfect, not because she failed to express her feelings in a thoughtful manner. His hurt reaction doesn't mean that she needed to stop her expression. What she must do after her expression is listen to his expression of his feelings. Even when our expression triggers an emotional reaction from others, all that we need to do is witness their expression. Thus we can avoid hurt feelings as emotional blackmail for interrupting honest communication. Handling these situations can prove to be very tricky.

In summary, all emotions are valid in and of themselves and absolutely subjective. Being okay with our feelings can help us change how we react in the future. While all feelings are valid, we can choose if and how to express our feelings and whether to let our feelings determine our behavior. Both repression and righteous justification are unhealthy responses to our emotions that keep us stuck in the same feelings. Being aware of our feelings and expressing them helps us to move through them with ease and grace; however, when expressing feelings we must do no harm and lovingly witness others' expression of their feelings.

Tool #5—Doing What Works

Craig came to me because he wanted to feel more confident when making presentations at work. As he told me a little about himself, we both realized that he was also having some problems in his marriage. He described how he was always doing things to please his wife, Nancy, but she never seemed satisfied with what he did. Even when he bought her a new car for her birthday, she became upset, saying it wasn't the model that she really wanted. He couldn't understand how she could be angry with him when he had been so generous. He then admitted that since this incident he's been withdrawn and distant from her. He said that he still loved Nancy, but being near her just made him feel so inadequate. "I feel like I can't ever do anything right."

When I asked him what it was like to be raised in his family, Craig told me that his now deceased alcoholic father would frequently come home drunk and physically abuse him. Craig never knew when his father would "go off" on him, and he lived in constant fear because his father's outbursts were random and unpredictable. His mother, he said, was a good woman who didn't deserve the treatment she got, and he still didn't understand why she never left his father.

Craig's history made sense to me. His background did not provide him with the skills for creating a healthy relationship with Nancy. Considering his personal history, Craig was doing a great job. After all, he was neither an alcoholic like his father nor abusive to his wife in any way. But not being abusive falls short of creating a healthy relationship. In truth, the skills he developed in order to survive in his very dysfunctional family of origin are exactly those behaviors that now prevent him from being more successful in his relationship with Nancy.

In Chapter Two, we learned how to get what we want in our relationships by making requests instead of complaining. In Chapter Three we learned that by fully expressing our appreciation we could increase the possibility that our requests would be heard as requests. Now we need to learn how to serve others in a way that they can get what they want in our relationships. This requires our moving beyond the old Golden Rule.

The old Golden Rule

The golden rule says that you should "do unto others as you would have others do unto you." For some, following this rule would vastly improve their relationships. It's certainly more compassionate than some other rules like "never give a sucker an even break" or "get them before they get you." But, even the golden rule falls short of always creating healthy and successful relationships. Instead, it's the perfect vehicle for projecting our needs and wants onto others while failing to truly understand what they really want and need.

Following the golden rule literally, we would do unto others what would meet *our* needs and wants. Unfortunately, our needs and others' needs may not match. In the extreme, the golden rule tells my daughter to buy my wife a "Barbie" doll for her birthday, fulfilling the golden rule perfectly. With the golden rule in mind, I wonder if season tickets to the local college basketball games might not be the perfect gift for my wife on our anniversary.

The problem

Sometimes the things we do in the positive spirit of the golden rule can cause serious problems. Most of us really do want to serve others, to do and say things that will please them; but with the golden rule encouraging us to project our own needs onto others, we're likely to fail.

We've all had the unpleasant experience of doing something that we thought would please someone, but didn't. Maybe you buy what you think will be the perfect gift for someone only to see the disappointment on his or her face as they pretend to be pleased with it. This can happen when we innocently project our needs and wants onto others instead of finding out what they really want. By not discovering what others truly want we can turn a well-intentioned action into an emotional disaster. Craig meant well when he bought Nancy a car for her birthday, but because it wasn't what she wanted, and after a long history of similar experiences, she couldn't even pretend to be happy. Caught off guard, Craig felt deeply hurt. We can easily empathize with Craig while also understanding why Nancy felt so upset with Craig, who had repeatedly missed the mark with her. Neither of them seems to be the culprit in this very real tragedy.

When this happens repeatedly in a relationship, everybody feels bad. In this instance, Craig feels unappreciated for what he did and inadequate, while Nancy feels misunderstood and unimportant. Their laments for this scenario could easily be "nothing I do is ever good enough" from Craig and "nobody really understands or cares about me" from Nancy.

The New Golden Rule

The solution to this dilemma is creating a new rule for relationships that states:

"Do for others what will fulfill the same *intention* as what you want others to do for you."

This New Golden Rule requires that we find out *exactly* what will fulfill a particular intention for someone. For example, if basketball tickets, a gift I would love to get, would make me feel loved, cared about and maybe even a little indulged on my birthday, then when picking a great birthday present for my wife, I need to find out exactly what will make *her* feel loved, cared about and maybe even a little indulged. Knowing her, this might be arranging a night out without our children. This could include flowers, champagne and room service in a hotel that has a sauna and indoor swimming pool, and later, back in the room, a good movie that we can watch while I massage her feet.

Discovering positive intentions

The new Golden Rule requires that we discover exactly what would satisfy the positive intentions we want to fulfill for others. So our first step is figuring out what those positive intentions are. Do we want them to be happy, or feel special or feel safe? We must use our understanding of others to decide what's important for them. For example, while excitement is important to my daughter, I know that for my best friend relaxation is a luxury. Notice, however, that excitement and relaxation are both intentions.

Intentions say nothing about how I might help them fulfill these intentions. Knowing what intentions are important to someone is the first step towards doing what will truly please them. But in order to be able to consistently fulfill others' intentions, we must clearly understand what intentions are.

Intentions are what something will accomplish or provide for someone. Whether something fulfills a particular intention is subjective. A present of a nice plant would please me but just be another burden to take care of for my wife. Feeling good is the evidence that something fulfills a positive intention. If Nancy had been happy when Craig gave her the car, he would know that he had done something that fulfilled some positive intention for her. We can all remember how good we've felt when our needs were met. When my daughters made cards for my birthday and told me how much they loved me, I felt loved and connected, important intentions for me.

Some intentions that we might help fulfill for others are security and safety, belonging, companionship, physical needs, feeling honored and respected, feeling important and worthwhile, feeling loved, feeling acknowledged and appreciated, and having fun. This is by no means a complete list. There are many others.

I'm not suggesting that we're responsible for meeting the needs of others. In truth, except for parental or guardian relationships, we are not inherently responsible for meeting others' needs. But an important part of any relationship is doing things for each other, so we might as well do things that help others feel good. Even though we're not inherently responsible for others' needs, we can often choose to contribute to those we care about. In the next chapter, I'll describe in more detail how to determine who is responsible for what in a relationship and how getting clear about our boundaries actually makes it easier for us to serve others.

Some Positive Intentions

1. Feeling secure and safe

2. Feeling connected

3. Feeling honored and respected

4. Feeling important and worthwhile

5. Feeling loved

6. Having fun

7. Physical comfort

8. Feeling appreciated

Fulfilling intentions

Once you know that you want to do something for someone and you have discovered what intentions you want to fulfill for them, your challenge becomes determining exactly what will fulfill these intentions. There are three ways to do this. First, you can pay attention. If you've been attentive in the past, then you will already know or have a good idea what will please somebody. If Craig had paid closer attention he might know what kind of car Nancy would like to have or even if she wanted a new car at all. If you have no clue about what would please someone, then either you haven't been paying attention or you haven't spent enough time together. Consistently disappointing others probably indicates that you've been projecting your own imagination, doing what you thought others would like rather than discovering what they really want. If this is the case, you must commit yourself to paying closer attention.

You can also use the second method — actually asking others what they would like and listening carefully to their response. Depending on your plans, you can ask directly or indirectly. The more indirect you are, the more you can surprise someone. On the other hand, when you're indirect you're more likely to miss the mark. Craig could have asked Nancy what kind of car she liked or invited her to join him in looking at cars. Asking, he might have discovered that she was fine with her present car and would rather use some of the money they would spend on a new car to take a special vacation and save the rest.

The third way is to consult with mutual friends and relatives. For my wife, I might ask my next door neighbor for advice. They are very close, so she probably has a good idea what my wife likes. Not only will I get some useful information, but I'll also probably get some recognition from my neighbor for being considerate and thoughtful.

As useful as the New Golden Rule is for these special occasions, it's even more helpful with the ordinary interactions of everyday life. How we behave in the mundane moments of life truly determines the health of our relationships. I can best serve our relationship by doing the little things that fulfill positive intentions for my wife every day. For example, I know that she appreciates my consulting with her before I make any significant time commitments to something new. Even though she rarely asks me to change my plans, she appreciates my consideration. When both of us actively serve each other, we both feel honored. This naturally leads to a greater willingness to serve others as well. Our relationship becomes a place where we feel nurtured and replenished, empowering us to go out into the world and more easily contribute to others.

Two inhibitions to serving others

Despite our good intentions, sometimes it's hard to serve. Past negative experiences can seriously inhibit our ability to serve others selflessly. Let me describe two types of experiences that can get in the way of our moving beyond the old golden rule.

NOT HAVING GOTTEN OUR OWN NEEDS MET

The assumption behind both the new and the old golden rule is that we want to serve others and provide them with some degree of happiness and pleasure. This requires directing our attention to the needs and wants of others. This can be a difficult task when we have unresolved past experiences of not having gotten our own needs met. These experiences can make us attend more to whether our own needs are being met and less to the needs of others. People who feel that their needs have not been met will find it hard to be freely giving to others. A history of not getting your needs met can create a sense of blind desperation. While in college, I volunteered to work with disadvantaged children. The first day with the children, I noticed that several of them would hide food in their pockets when they thought no one was looking, even though there was more than enough food for everyone. When I pointed this out to my supervisor, she told me that children with a history of real hunger, those with experiences of not having had enough to eat sometime in their lives, would hoard food against some future possibility of being without food. She told me that even when there was a set amount for everyone, when there was only one apple for each child at snack time for example, these children would try to hoard without concern for whether the other children got any. In the same way, those of us with some experience of being emotionally starved can become obsessed with getting our own emotional needs met, while ignoring the needs of others.

Moving beyond attending solely to our own needs requires that we resolve these past experiences by fully processing them. As we discussed in the last chapter, completing an experience means identifying it and then acknowledging and expressing our feelings. By completing these experiences we will heal old wounds, freeing ourselves to attend to the wishes and needs of others, without being so preoccupied with our own.

PAST FAILURES IN MEETING THE NEEDS OF OTHERS

The experience of never or rarely meeting others' needs successfully will make us hesitate to try again. Craig is hesitant to give anything else to Nancy because of his failures in the past. In some way, all of us, especially those raised in severely dysfunctional families, have experienced people who are close to us behaving in inconsistent and even unpredictable ways. In these families, it's hard, if not impossible, to predict what will please someone because the same behavior will get different responses. One day we are praised for speaking up and the next day we are yelled at for "sticking our two cents in where it does not belong."

This creates an interesting bind. On the one hand, we really want to please others because we haven't been able to please others in the past. On the other hand, we're hesitant because of our past failures. Craig's history with his unpredictably violent father makes him want to please his wife, yet hesitant to do what is necessary to succeed. He wants to please Nancy, but because of his past failure he doesn't trust her response.

With each experience of failure we become more afraid to risk trying to fulfill the needs of others and eventually we don't even bother to make the attempt. Even when we do try, we can feel so preoccupied with our own fears and bad feelings from the past that we can't bring enough of our attention to the situation to gather the information needed to decide how to best serve others. Once again we fail to meet someone's needs, creating even more evidence for the self-fulfilling prophecy that we're incapable of making others feel good.

The failure of mind-reading

When we have consistently failed to fulfill the wishes and needs of others, getting it right the first time becomes extremely important. So instead of looking to others to tell us what they need or want — because this never worked for us in the past anyway — we turn inward and engage in an internal process of mind-reading. We try to guess what will please others and hope that we can conjure up what will work. Because of his past experience, Craig treats Nancy as if she were his father, who was consistently unpredictable, by trying to imagine what would please her without asking her. When he predictably failed again because he did not get the information he needed from Nancy, he adds to his pile of evidence that he's not very good at pleasing others. This failure only reinforces his tendency to mind-read in the future.

Even though our intention when we mind-read others is to serve them, mind-reading is incredibly egocentric. When we mind-read, we're directing our attention inward as we egocentrically attend to our own need to avoid punishment and ignore others' real needs. We're so preoccupied with our own fear and hurt that we're unable to learn what others need from us. People who mind-read complain that others don't appreciate their selfless giving but are unwittingly only concerned with their own needs and fears. However, to create healthy relationships we must get our focus off our own needs and move beyond mind-reading.

Moving beyond mind-reading

The solution to our unintentional, egocentric mind-reading is performing the truly selfless act of recovering our memories of being abused and neglected. Then after fully processing them by recognizing, accepting and, if necessary, expressing our feelings, we can forgive all those involved including our parents and ourselves. This is no simple feat. However, fully processing these old experiences frees our attention from our past hurt and redirects it to others in the present. Having healed our past, we can recreate our present relationships in the light of forgiving and service. We can direct our attention to the needs and wants of others, not because we're afraid, but because we love them and desire to create healing relationships that serve everyone.

If Craig works through the pain of his horrible experiences with his dad, he will be able to perceive how he has learned to use mind-reading as an adaptation to his childhood. He can then learn to take the risk of asking Nancy what she wants because he knows that she is not his father and is likely to be more predictable and appreciative of his desire to please her.

Taking the risk of making mistakes

In attempting to please others you must be willing to make mistakes, a difficult task if you've learned that making mistakes is unacceptable. If this is the case, you need to take time to heal your emotional wounds from not having been allowed to make mistakes because these wounds greatly increase our present emotional risk. When Craig failed to please Nancy with the car, he became overwhelmed with feelings of inadequacy and helplessness. Without healing his old wounds, the risk of failing in the present also includes the risk of feeling all these unresolved hurt feelings from his past. In contrast, once he works through much of this old hurt, he won't feel as bad when he makes a mistake. Feeling more resourceful, he'll be able to stay present, learn from his mistakes and act more effectively in the future.

Feedback, not failure

Mistakes are an important part of learning. The most empowering attitude we can take towards our mistakes is to perceive them as feedback that will help us decide what to do in the future. A useful phrase to define this attitude is:

"There is no failure, only feedback."

We transform mistakes into feedback when we realize that failure is an unnecessary judgment that we assign to mistakes. Judging is something we do at the end of an activity, therefore, judging our mistakes by treating them as failures is saying that the process is done. However, if we feel committed to improving, our learning continues and the process is never done. Our mistakes become feedback that shapes the changes we can make to improve. All our judgments are premature when we consider mistakes feedback because we always have another opportunity to get it right. When Craig judged Nancy's reaction as failure, he began to withdraw and eventually gave up trying to please her. But if, instead, he took her reaction as feedback, he could figure out what he could do differently in the future. Even if they ended their marriage, Craig could learn important lessons from his mistakes, learning that will help him in his next relationship.

Treating mistakes as feedback, not failure, is a lot like being good at darts. Whenever I throw a dart that misses the target, I use this feedback to adjust my aim or technique. The only difference is the importance we assign to making a mistake. A mistake when throwing darts is usually not as important to us as mistakes in our relationships. We tend to judge quickly when we feel that the stakes are high. However, we need to take the exact opposite approach. When the stakes are high, when we're attempting something that is important to us, is exactly when we need to treat mistakes as feedback. When we're doing something that's important to us, we need the resourcefulness of being able to take feedback and use our feedback to improve. It's no big deal if I give up on a game of darts, or even if I never play darts again. Giving up on a relationship *is* a big deal, and we deserve to be as resourceful as we can be when trying to make our relationships work.

In contrast, treating our mistakes as failure makes us feel bad and does not help us improve. Drawn inward by bad feelings from past failures and our inability to successfully separate who we are from what we do, we are likely to indulge in an orgy of self-criticism. Our energy goes toward mentally beating ourselves up instead of planning what to do in the future, and we feel too bad to get the feedback that might help us succeed.

We're never bad for having attempted something from our good intentions. We actually deserve to be acknowledged for our attempt. Having the courage to continue in the face of our mistakes is a statement that we feel so committed to having healthy relationships that we will continue to work at our relationships in spite of our mistakes, taking them as feedback that helps us to improve.

Becoming responsive by not taking things personally

In addition to treating mistakes as feedback, we need to understand that how others respond to us is not personal to us. When others respond differently than we hoped, it's common to take their reaction personally, taking it to mean something about us. Suppose my wife isn't thrilled with my gift of a night away from the children — if I take it personally I make it mean that she doesn't love and appreciate me or that she thinks I'm a thoughtless, insensitive oaf. When I take her response personally, I make her response about me, not about her.

At most, her response means that she didn't like my gift. Realizing that her response is personal to her, not me, actually frees me to be more responsive to her. Her personal makeup, her feelings, thoughts, personal history and model of the world all determine her response. Her response is feedback for me and thus provides information I can use to make better choices in the future. In addition, getting a response that I didn't anticipate will motivate me to find out why she responded the way she did. If my wife doesn't like my gift of a night away, I need to find out why so that I can better understand her. This can only enhance our relationship.

Not taking her response personally, I become empowered to be responsive to her without feeling responsible for her reaction. Being "responsive to" rather than feeling "responsible for" her response allows me to notice her reaction and then use my "mistake" as feedback for learning how to better serve her in the future. I can still choose to be responsive to her reaction even though it's not personal to me.

In the next chapter, I will discuss in more detail those relationship boundaries that indicate who is responsible for what. That discussion will help you understand more clearly how you can do something that gets a negative reaction from someone and not feel responsible for that reaction, while continuing to be responsive

Using the New Golden Rule

1. Determine the positive intention(s) you want to fulfill

2. Explore what will fulfill this positive intention by:

   A. *Examining the past for clues*

   B. *Asking directly what will fulfill this intention*

   C. *Consulting with friends and relatives*

3. Put the plan into action

4. Understand that:

   A. *It's okay to make a mistake*

   B. *How someone responds to your gestures is not personal*

The other side of the New Golden Rule: responding to intention

We can help others feel free to risk doing things that might not hit the mark with us by recognizing and appreciating their good intentions for us. Acknowledging and trusting that the people we love act and communicate from basic good intentions for us creates room for them to make mistakes. People will take risks when they know that the relationship is not at stake with everything they do or say. When my wife acknowledges our daughter's good intention in buying her a Barbie doll, she reinforces our daughter's desire to be giving to others. If on the other hand my wife fails to recognize her good intention, expressing only disappointment, our daughter will become more hesitant to give to her. She will become "gun shy" about taking this risk of making a mistake.

Acknowledging others' good intentions creates an open and loving environment. Our acknowledgment helps others feel competent and resourceful, and they become much more open to feedback and suggestions. Feeling appreciated, they will hear these suggestions as requests and not criticism. In this cooperative atmosphere, we eventually get what we want and they get to feel the satisfaction of providing happiness and pleasure. If Nancy could have acknowledged Craig for his good intentions in buying her a car, she also could have helped him learn how to get the information he would need to make good choices in their future together.

What to do when good intentions are not evident

Good intentions are not always evident. Perceiving good intention when someone is being physically or emotionally abusive to us is extremely difficult. In these situations, people are acting out of their fear and insecurity, and our well-being takes a back seat to their self-protective impulses. They might not really be in any danger, but they feel that they are, and that fear grabs all their attention.

When you feel consistently abused or mistreated in a relationship, the first step is to get it stopped. The next step is to look more closely and notice if there is any good intention for you behind their behavior. If there is, you can try to redirect this good intention. The husband who is critical of his wife might only want her to have a better life. The fact that his approach isn't working doesn't deny his misguided good intention. In this situation it might be useful to get some professional help. Outside help can often facilitate redirecting good intention in a relationship. A professional will be able to fan the flames of good intention and help create healthy ways to express it.

When it seems impossible to redirect good intention or there really seems to be no good intention behind someone's treatment of you, it's time to reevaluate whether to continue a relationship. Being aware that someone has a great deal of pain that inhibits their ability to act out of good intentions makes leaving them a difficult decision. On one hand, you stay because you understand their pain but possibly subject yourself to further mistreatment. On the other hand, you leave but know that underneath they are really not bad. There is no right choice. Whether you want to continue to be intimately involved with another is a personal decision. You can choose to stay and help with someone's healing, choose to step back with your heart open because of the damage being done to you and other loved ones or decide to postpone any final decision.

There's no objectively good reason for a particular choice. There is only your subjective decision. This is also not a moral choice, but one of personal consideration and ethics. You only need to live with whatever you decide to do.

I am not advocating bailing out of all relationships when they get a little rough; I'm just pointing out that true responsibility is making free choices, not behaving out of some perceived obligation or duty. However, taking responsibility for making conscious choices ensures that our relationships remain alive and free.

Relationships work when we can do those things that successfully fulfill the needs and importantly held intentions of those we love. They feel honored, considered and valued, while we feel competent and needed. Our relationships thrive when we serve each other from our good intentions and when we receive from our awareness of others' good intentions for us.

Earlier in this chapter, I discussed how not taking things personally empowers us to be responsive to others without being responsible. We can best do this by establishing and maintaining clear boundaries.

Tool #6—Setting Boundaries

When Marie, 37, came to see me, she was in a panic about a family reunion she was supposed to attend in about a month. She was from a rural southern home where family was very important. Recently, however, she had begun to recover memories of being sexually abused by an uncle who would also be at the reunion. At first, she doubted her memories, questioning whether she wasn't merely reacting to something she had seen about child abuse on one of the talk shows, but she soon discovered that two of her cousins also remembered being abused by this same uncle. She didn't know what to do. She'd always been a good daughter, visiting her mother frequently and willingly fulfilling her family obligations. When she told her mother about her recovered memories, her mother didn't confirm or deny their truth, saying instead, that if these things happened, it was a long time ago and she needed to get on with her life. Marie felt betrayed and abandoned by her mother at the time, and she still felt angry with her. She told me that, on the one hand, she didn't feel like going to the reunion, experiencing panic attacks whenever she thought about seeing her uncle there; on the other hand, she felt guilty about disappointing her mother, who couldn't understand why Marie didn't want to go.

Marie had a shaky history with men. She had been married for several years in her twenties to an alcoholic who verbally abused her. And her only long-term relationship since leaving him had been with a married man, who, for years, promised to leave his wife and marry her, but never did. She eventually let him go and hadn't been in a relationship for more than four years. By the time she came for therapy, even the idea of being in an intimate relationship terrified her.

I realized that most of my work with Marie would be to help her distinguish, establish and maintain clear boundaries in her life. When she first came to me, she was unable to take care of herself without feeling guilty for hurting others' feelings. Lacking the ability to establish emotionally safe limits for herself and not trusting her own sense of things, she felt that she had no right to make choices without her mother's approval

As we mature and begin to differentiate ourselves from others, our psychological health requires that we learn how to protect our individuality at the same time that we engage others in mutually healthy ways. Boundaries are an essential component of all healthy relationships because they define and protect our individuality. In this chapter, I will describe the three types of boundaries, our problems with boundaries and how to establish and maintain healthy boundaries. I will also offer a detailed discussion of how we can teach our children about boundaries. It's a lot easier to learn how to maintain and establish healthy boundaries when you're young than to have to unlearn old bad habits before learning new ones. Also, the challenge of teaching children about boundaries helps us clear up our own confusion about boundaries.

Three types of boundaries

The **first type of boundary** assigns responsibility in relationships. It defines **who is responsible for what**. But in order to know who is responsible for what, we must first know what there is to be responsible for. Earlier, we learned that we have three forms of expression and experience.

These are behavior or doing (both voluntary and involuntary), thinking and feeling. All human expression and experiences fall under one or more of these categories. There is nothing else. For example, in my relationship with you, there is what I do, think and feel, and what you do, think and feel. That's all there is.

This first type of boundary delineates that I'm responsible for what I do, think and feel, and you're responsible for what you do, think and feel. This seems very simple, but sometimes it's hard to be clear about who is responsible for what, especially when our behavior affects another's feelings. For example, if Marie were to not attend her family reunion, she would probably feel responsible for her mother's subsequent disappointment. Like Marie, many of us learned as children to feel responsible for our parents' feelings. If we did things that disappointed them, we felt responsible for their feelings of disappointment.

The **second type of boundary** is limits. Limits define **what we are willing to do and what we're not willing to do.** Each of us is responsible for setting our own limits and living with the ramifications of our decisions. Marie has the right to choose to not attend her family reunion because she doesn't feel emotionally ready to handle it. However, if she chooses to stay home, she must live with her mother being disappointed with her and with not being able to spend time with those relatives she would like to see.

Deciding what we're willing and not willing to do shapes our lives. When I was out of school for a few years, I decided that I was no longer willing to work for a social service organization with its inherent constraints. I was, however, willing to take the risk of starting a private psychotherapy practice against the advice of many of my friends and colleagues. My decision greatly affected my future. My career has been very different from what it would have been if I had continued to work in agencies. I've had a lot more freedom, but when I want to have some contact with colleagues I need to make an intentional effort. I've been able to be more successful financially, but I've had to live with the uncertainty of not having a guaranteed salary.

The **third type of boundary** sets **the degree of intimacy or closeness that we're willing to have with particular others.** There are things about my life that I would share with my wife that I would not share with my neighbor, and things I would share with my neighbor that I wouldn't share with my mail carrier. Marie felt more comfortable sharing her process of healing with her cousins than she did with her mother who wasn't as understanding of what she'd gone through. This type of boundary determines with whom we share our lives, our involvement with others. We each have the right to choose whom to include in our lives and thus define our own circle of intimacy.

We each have the right to establish personal boundaries that respect our personal desires, needs and comfort. Except in guardian relationships, no one has the right to set boundaries for someone else. It's appropriate and desirable for responsible adults to set boundaries for children or other wards, but adults have the right to define their own boundaries. Later in the chapter, I will discuss how to thoughtfully set boundaries for children.

The Three Types of Boundaries

1. **Responsibility** — who is responsible for what.
   Everyone is responsible for their own actions, thoughts and feelings.

2. **Limits** — what we are willing and not willing to do.

3. **Intimacy** — how closely involved we wish to be with particular others.

The source of our confusion with boundaries

Sometimes, setting and maintaining boundaries can be confusing because we haven't had enough opportunity to learn about setting healthy boundaries. Most of us were raised in families where boundaries were often unclear and inconsistent. Also, as children others set boundaries for us and we had little opportunity to gradually learn how to set boundaries for ourselves. Consequently, those of us who learned to look to others to set boundaries for us can now find it hard to take responsibility for the difficult decisions in our lives.

I do not, however, recommend blaming our parents. The concept of boundaries is a relatively new one and our parents didn't have access to such a concept. They were concerned with our safety and with providing for us, and we were lucky if they happened to provide us with an environment in which we could learn about boundaries. Instead of blaming our parents, we need to take the time now to learn about boundaries and how to use them.

A lot of the confusion about boundaries concerns knowing who is responsible for what. As I stated earlier, in our relationship I am responsible for my thoughts, feelings and actions and you are responsible for your thoughts, feelings and actions. This is straightforward. However, many of us feel that we're at least partially responsible for the thoughts, actions and most often the feelings of others, while some of us go through life assigning the responsibility for our actions, thoughts and feelings to everyone else.

Being responsible for the feelings of others

It's easy to learn that you are responsible for others' feelings. When parents are overreactive to small problems or don't talk about their feelings, their children learn to feel responsible for their moods and feelings. When parents virtually become upset over spilt milk, feeling responsible for their unhappiness follows. In my own life, I noticed that if I got good grades in school and did what my parents told me to do, they'd be happy. When I did something wrong, they became unhappy. Being young and a magical thinker, that is thinking that I had more power than I really had, I started to think that I could make them happy. Eventually, I began to base my decisions on whether what I did would make them happy. Merely choosing to please them, however, wouldn't be a problem in and of itself, but I felt that I was personally responsible for their happiness.

We are *not* responsible for the feelings of others. Believing that we are disempowers us and all those whose responsibilities we usurp. By being responsible for her mother's disappointment, Marie is saying that her mother can't handle her own feelings. Taking responsibility for my parents' feelings is a statement that I believe that they aren't capable of being responsible for and handling them. I may think that I'm taking care of them, but I'm really only preventing them from learning how to handle their own feelings.

Being aware of all our various feelings, especially those that don't feel good, is an important part of being fully alive. When we habitually protect people from their negative feelings, we rob them of their full experience of life and rob ourselves of the full expression of our aliveness.

Being considerate of others' feelings

Allowing others to be responsible for their own feelings doesn't mean we can't consider others' feelings in our decisions. What we must avoid is feeling that we have the bottom-line responsibility for their feelings. We can influence others' feelings, but they are ultimately responsible for them.

There is a high cost for taking responsibility for others' feelings. When we *have* to take responsibility for others' feelings, we cannot *choose* to be considerate of their feelings. Conversely, only when we know that we aren't responsible for others' feelings can we truly consider their feelings. Only when Marie feels that she has the right to let her mother feel disappointed with her decision, that she does not *have* to change her decision in order to make her mother feel better, will she be free to consider her mother's wishes. She can then weigh her mother's wishes against her needs before making a decision. Only when she knows that it's okay if she doesn't can she choose to attend her family reunion as a gift to her mother. Therefore, the course of our therapy together was to first give her permission to respect her own feelings and not go, then to help her give her mother the space to feel disappointed without Marie feeling guilty. With this permission, Marie realized that she would really like to go as a gift to her mother, so we began to work on helping her freely choose to attend the reunion.

Creating healthy relationships through sharing

If we're not responsible for others feelings, then what is our responsibility? Actually, beyond our *own* feelings, thoughts and actions we aren't responsible for anything. However, being responsible for our own feelings, thoughts and actions falls one step short of being in relationship. Relationship occurs when we attend fully to the expression of another's feelings, thoughts and actions, and freely express our own. Relationship is sharing what is going on for us and witnessing others' sharing.

Not being clear about who is responsible for what inhibits both our expression and our ability to pay attention to others' sharing. When we feel responsible for others' feelings we inhibit our own expression because we fear hurting them. We filter our behavior through our obsession with whether we are hurting others, becoming more and more paralyzed. Until Marie understands that she is only responsible for her decision to not attend the reunion and not responsible for her mother's disappointment, Marie will feel obligated to go. She automatically does what she's always done. Our constant attention to whether others are being hurt by our actions also interrupts our ability to listen and witness their expression. We are so preoccupied with whether we are hurting others' feelings that we can never truly attend to and freely honor their expression. Unable to accept her mother's disappointment, Marie makes her mother's disappointment about herself and doesn't really honor her mother's feelings. In contrast, when she understands that her mother is responsible for her own feelings, she will be able to respectfully honor and witness her mother's expression of her disappointment.

I'm not saying that we should share everything that comes into our heads — though I've known some people who would like to. Actually, when we free up our expression by no longer holding ourselves responsible for others' feelings, we can more thoughtfully decide what's worth sharing. When we inhibit our expression because we're afraid to hurt others' feelings, we never feel fully expressed and can ironically feel a constant need to express. We've all known people who say a lot but rarely share anything that seems very important or intimate. Our challenge is to share ourselves in ways that respect others but allows them to take responsibility for their reactions to us.

How we learned to be responsible for others' feelings

More fully understanding how we learned to feel responsible for others' feelings can help us to stop. Examining our early experiences and the decisions we made at the time can lead us to new decisions that will support our creating and maintaining healthier boundaries.

Most of us first learned about boundaries in families where boundaries were not clear. Because we depended on our parents for our well-being, and how they treated us depended on how they felt, we learned to pay very close attention to whether or not they felt happy. Unfortunately, without the open and free discussion of who was responsible for what, we easily assumed that we were responsible for our parents' feelings. We might have noticed, for example, that our parents got happy when we received good grades and unhappy when we received poor ones. Then, being naturally egocentric, as all children are, we easily took responsibility for their feelings of happiness and unhappiness.

It's not a big jump from taking responsibility for our parents' happiness to shaping our behavior to influence their feelings. I'm not saying that parents shouldn't have feelings about what their children do; just understand that your children will perceive this as a good reason to take responsibility for your feelings. Parents are not responsible for their children doing this, and they can't prevent it from occurring. It's something that occurs naturally in all families. The best we can do, as parents, is create an environment that is open to discussing and correcting any boundary problems.

Letting go of our responsibility for others' feelings

Taking responsibility for others' feelings costs us aliveness, self-expression and intimacy. When we're too concerned with not hurting others' feelings, we inhibit our own expression. If we think that some action or statement might hurt someone's feelings, we suppress it. We fail to express ourselves fully because we fear hurting them, consequently hiding things that might actually create more intimacy if we shared them. Marie tries to keep her mother happy by suppressing her own needs and limiting her expression of herself around her mother. When she first came to see me, she was already feeling alienated from her mother and spending less time with her. She said that she just couldn't be herself around her mother.

When we finally realize that the cost of protecting others' feelings is too high, we can begin to change by exploring how we arrived at our beliefs. We need to remember how we learned to protect others from their painful feelings and release any incomplete feelings and thoughts related to these experiences. Then we can make new decisions about others' capabilities and our responsibility to them. Completing these experiences creates space for new and healthier beliefs that support our being fully self-expressed, sharing ourselves freely and openly witnessing each other's expression. Marie was able to remember in our work together that her mother had always had a hard time dealing with conflicts and problems. Whenever there was a problem her mother would get hysterical and angry. Marie learned not to say things that would disturb her mother, repressing her self-expression and eventually developing the sense that there was no room for her to be herself around her mother. She felt unimportant, alone and abandoned, feelings that persisted to the present day. Eventually though, with dedicated work in therapy, she was able to express and release her feelings, forgive her mother and herself and create room for a new, healthier relationship.

How to help our children learn about boundaries

Teaching our children about boundaries is as important as learning how to set and maintain healthy boundaries for ourselves. If we teach our children about boundaries, they will approach relationships with more comfort and courage. They will have the ability to assign responsibility appropriately and be able to fully participate in and contribute to their relationships.

I know of two ways to help our children learn about healthy boundaries. The first is taking responsibility for our own actions, thoughts and feelings. The second is providing children with a safe environment for gradually learning to establish and maintain all three types of boundaries for themselves.

Taking responsibility for our actions, thoughts and feelings

Clearly communicating to our children will help them avoid taking responsibility for our actions, thoughts and particularly our feelings. When we talk freely about our thoughts, feelings, and experience, we let them know that we, not they, are responsible for them.

When we feel bad, we need to let our children know what's bothering us and that they're not responsible for making us happy. By discussing how we feel with our children, we demonstrate how to accept uncomfortable feelings and that expressing feelings helps us move through them. We need to share all kinds of feelings with our children. When we do, they learn that painful feelings aren't bad and that it's okay to express good feelings. We can talk about how they can feel compassionate for us when we feel bad without needing to do something to make us feel better and that the best thing they can do when we feel bad is love us anyway.

Of course, doing the same for them when they feel bad is the best way for them to learn. When my daughter feels upset about not getting the part she wanted in a performance, I need to listen and understand how she feels. I don't need to rush into telling her what she can do to improve in the future. Feeling supported by me, she'll be more willing to ask for my help when she's ready to think about how she could do better in the future. By listening, I'm letting her know that how she does is not as important to me as how she feels about herself and her experience.

With older children, we can even have discussions about boundaries including how to make decisions about taking responsibility. We can talk with them about how to balance our concerns for others' needs with our own and share how hard it is to sit by and let someone feel bad without rushing to make them feel better. We can talk about how much easier we make it for all of us when we share what is going on for us instead of acting it out. After all, it's much easier on my family when I tell them that I've had a hard day instead of just being irritable and short-tempered.

Talking freely about our actions, thoughts and feelings creates an environment where our children feel free to express themselves. They learn to be comfortable with the expression of feelings without needing to make others feel better by taking a responsibility that is not theirs. When they go out in the world, they're better prepared to make healthy relationship choices. They then become attracted to people who are also willing to be responsible for their own actions and experience.

Providing a safe environment for gradual learning

Besides modeling that we can intelligently and thoughtfully establish and maintain all three forms of boundaries, we can best teach our children how to establish and maintain healthy boundaries by providing them with opportunities to establish boundaries and make choices for themselves. However, this learning must be gradual.

When our children are small, we set boundaries for them to keep them safe and help them learn that the world is a safe place. We empower them to gradually explore and learn how to make their own choices and decisions about boundaries. I've noticed that those children who feel safest when very young are most capable of exploring and taking the risks of making choices for themselves as they grow older. We've all seen specials on TV where the young monkey alternates exploring her environment with going back to nestle in the comfort of her mother.

Our challenge in gradually transferring responsibility for setting and maintaining boundaries to our children is balancing safety with providing them with the opportunity to learn. The two mistakes we can make are giving children too much responsibility at too young an age and not giving them enough responsibility when they're ready to handle it. By both of these mistakes, children fail to learn that they can trust their ability to set boundaries for themselves.

When we give children too much responsibility at too young an age, they feel unsafe and unable to set their own

limits. Exposing children to risks and mature choices at too
early an age only makes them fearful and afraid, and eventually leads to the belief that the world is an unsafe place.
Being afraid in an unsafe world can create two problems.
First, believing the world is unsafe, they will eventually
make choices and act in ways that will continually recreate
what they believe to be true. Those who believe that the
world is unsafe make decisions that lead to danger and thus
realize their self-fulfilling prophecy. Secondly, young children who have too much freedom and responsibility
become overwhelmed. They often react by behaving imma-
turely, trying to go back to a "safer" time when they didn't
have so much to handle. They regress and try to give
responsibility for their lives back to their parents, feeling
too afraid to handle their own lives. Such children tend to
have more difficulty transitioning to the next level of development, whether it's not wanting to go to school or
engaging in "baby talk".

When we don't provide opportunities for children to
learn how to take responsibility for their lives, they fail to
learn that they can take care of themselves. When we try to
protect our children too much by making all their decisions
beyond the age when they can begin to make decisions for
themselves, they never learn how to make intelligent choices. We deny them the opportunity to learn from their
mistakes before the risks are very big. Thrusting them out
in the world without having practiced setting boundaries at
home is like trying to learn how to hit a baseball in the
World Series. Just as young ballplayers first learn to hit off
a tee with plenty of coaching to help them, children need
to learn about setting and maintaining healthy boundaries
gradually in the home. There, they can get the help they

need from parents and older siblings, experience gradual success and make mistakes in a forgiving environment.

Human beings don't come with operating manuals, so there are no absolute guidelines for how to gradually introduce children to becoming responsible. We can, however, watch closely as they learn how to handle increasing amounts of responsibility. As they succeed at one level, we can give them more responsibility. If they don't handle it, we can help them by sharing their load or working with them to learn how. Creating a gradual learning process and attending to how well they do gives us the flexibility to adjust things accordingly at any time.

Learning about each type of boundary

Let's consider how we can gradually teach our children to set and maintain each form of boundary. Just like adults, children are responsible for their thoughts and feelings. How they think and feel is up to them. We can, however, teach them desirable ways to express these thoughts and feelings. For example, we can teach our children to verbalize their anger instead of striking out violently at other people.

Because young children are innocent, we must support them by sharing responsibility for what they do. When our daughters were very small, my wife and I "baby-proofed" our house, putting things that we didn't want broken out of their reach. We didn't expect them to be able to stay away from things that might break until they were old enough to comfortably handle this responsibility without a lot of reminding. Our responsibility as adults is to recognize what each of our children can handle at a certain age and gradually provide them with the opportunity. We share responsibility with them for their actions as they grow until they learn to act responsibly. We take responsibility for keeping our younger children out of the street until they learn to look for cars and not play in busy streets. As we gradually relinquish our responsibility for our children, they learn to be more responsible for themselves.

Our primary concerns with limits are safety and emotional well-being. As children mature, they gradually need more and more freedom to make their own choices about what they're able and willing to handle in their lives. When my children were young, I wanted to meet the parents of my daughters' friends before we allowed them to spend the night at their home. I trust my teenager to judge for herself whether it's safe for her to stay over a friend's house. She has successfully demonstrated to us that she can be thoughtful about these decisions and will talk to us if she has a problem. As they increasingly demonstrate the ability to handle the responsibilities we have given them, we can give our children more responsibility. There are no hard and fast rules for this. Decisions need to be subjective because children are different and they each mature at the rate that's exactly right for them. Gradually allowing them to set their own limits prepares them gracefully for the transition into adulthood when they will be making their own decisions as a rule and consulting with their parents only on rare occasions.

Our major concern in choosing whom we allow to get close to our children is safety. We have the right to set these boundaries for our children when someone clearly seems to be dangerous or potentially a negative influence. However, we must be careful to get enough information before doing this. How people dress or cut their hair doesn't necessarily determine their character. We should make these difficult decisions with our children in an open and communicative environment. We can take more license to decide what adults are around our children and let our children pick their own friends. They will anyway. Rarely is it necessary to forbid a friendship. We are much better off, particularly with teenagers, expressing our opinion and letting them make their own decisions about their friends. Feeling supported in this way, our teenagers will be more likely to talk to us if they have a problem. Trusting someone is always the best way to help them learn to be trustworthy.

As important as not letting children be close to people who are dangerous or serious negative influences is respecting our children's right to choose to be distant from someone. Even the smallest infant has good instincts about who is safe and who is not. We need to respect their wisdom. If a friend wants to hold one of my children but my child doesn't want him to hold her, I don't force or try to convince her that she should. She gets the important message that I respect her and that her wishes count. She learns that she has the right to set intimacy boundaries for herself. As a bonus, I can trust that as an adult she won't become involved with someone because of some misguided sense of obligation.

How we communicate our concerns about boundaries to our children depends on their maturity. A very young child may not have the capacity to understand our reasoning, but as children grow older we can verbalize our concerns and reasoning with them and arrive at choices cooperatively. Rare situations may call for us to make a dictatorial decision, but there is certainly room for a great deal of discussion before such a drastic measure. The exceptions are physically dangerous situations that require immediate action. It's appropriate and desirable for me to decide to stop my two-year old daughter from running out into traffic.

In the process of helping our children learn about boundaries we will be recreating our own life, helping create a world where individuals feel honored and fully able to contribute freely to others. We will be healing old wounds that have prevented our attending to others and sharing our lives with those we love, thus creating a world where we can live cooperatively and lovingly with all others and all living things.

Keys to Teaching Our Children How to Set and Maintain Boundaries

1. Balance safety and providing children with the opportunity to learn.

2. Provide opportunities for children to practice setting boundaries.

3. Gradually increase the amount of responsibility they have.

4. Demonstrate setting and maintaining healthy boundaries for yourself.

Only when we have clear boundaries that define our individuality can we freely and fully relate to each other. When we know and respect each other's responsibility, we can choose to be freely responsive to each other. Without clear boundaries, we are just reliving a past that might not have been so great the first time around.

When we clearly define our boundaries we can more easily witness and validate others' expression. As we stop taking responsibility for others' feelings, we experience the birth of our true compassion and caring. Not taking responsibility for others' feelings, we can choose to be compassionate and understanding of their experience. True compassion depends on freedom of choice and only occurs when others truly honor our boundaries with open hearts. Only then are we truly free to serve others. When we define our boundaries well we can even choose to be self sacrificing. Having chosen freely and taken responsibility for our own actions, we are not martyrs but giving freely of what we have to give. Ultimately as we all learn to create and maintain clear boundaries, we will free up boundless energy that we've been wasting in our "soap opera dramas." We can then redirect this energy toward solving the seemingly hopeless problems that face us now, like saving the Earth from a polluted death and ending hunger.

In this chapter I've discussed the three types of boundaries and how to teach our children to establish clear boundaries for themselves. However, in order to be responsive to others by being clear about boundaries, we first need to know what others are thinking and feeling. This requires not only telling the truth to each other but also being straight.

Tool #7—Being Straight

Jill, 37, was referred by her physical therapist because her chronic back pain following a car accident was not responding to treatment. After months of physical therapy, she was still experiencing a lot of pain, and her physician and physical therapist could no longer find any physiological basis for it. They knew that I'd had some success working with chronic pain patients and that I could at least help her learn to cope with the pain. When she first came, she said that she knew that there was more going on for her than just the physical problem. Using a technique I'd developed for discovering the emotional component of physical problems, I was able to help her identify some strong emotions that she'd been suppressing.

Recently, she had discovered that she couldn't have children, so she had begun to explore the option of adopting a child. However, a few months into this process her husband, who was 45, told her that he didn't want to adopt and that, since he was getting older, he wasn't sure that he wanted to have children at all. After limited discussion, she agreed to give up her dream of a family because she "couldn't make him do something he didn't want to do." She reported that she felt disappointed at first, but "got over it" pretty quickly. In our work together, she realized that she'd repressed some very strong feelings about her husband's unilateral decision, and she still felt very upset about not being able to have a family. She also recognized that, feeling distant from her husband, she'd been gradually withdrawing from him.

With my encouragement, and after validating her feelings herself, she talked to her husband about them. She told him that she felt disappointed about not having a family and angry that he had come to his decision without discussing it with her first. To her surprise, he was open to hearing her and even acknowledged her for sharing her feelings with him. He'd noticed the growing distance between them and was glad to be reconnecting with her. As it turned out, he wasn't firm in his decision to not have children, and they've reopened the discussion. Within weeks of this discussion, her pain was almost completely gone.

A guaranteed way to sabotage any relationship is to be dishonest. Another way to sabotage a relationship is to not be straightforward. Here's an example that illustrates the difference between being honest and being straight. Let's say that I feel angry with my wife for not calling me when she was out of town, and that I also feel mildly annoyed with her because she left a mess in the living room. Exploding with anger over the messy living room, ranting and raving about how "she never does the things I ask her to do," is an example of being honest without being straight. I felt honestly annoyed about the messy room but expressed my annoyance with the much greater anger attached to her failure to call me. I was being honest but not candid with her. Faced with this raving lunatic, she accuses me of "overreacting," and of course she's right because I wasn't straight about what was really bothering me.

Healthy relationships require that we be both honest and straight with each other. Being straight means expressing what is most important to us with the emotional intensity that goes with it. There are three ways we can avoid being straight with each other. First is repressing our feelings from one situation, then displacing our feelings by overreacting to another. Second is not sharing those thoughts, which, if shared, would make an important difference in our relationships. Third is withholding, not

sharing something that affects how we act in our relationships. In this chapter, I will address being straight about
our feelings and thoughts. I will address withholding in the
next chapter.

Learning to hide our feelings

When those around me are saying things like "I don't have
any idea what's bothering Alan" or "what's got into him" I
can be pretty certain that I'm displacing feelings. I also
know that I'm displacing feelings when I'm overreactive.
When I yell at the dog for licking my hand as I walk by,
then I need to figure out what's really bothering me.

Usually, not being totally straight about our feelings
results from not being fully aware of what we're feeling.
Not knowing what we feel is rooted in our culture —
including our families and the society at large — that con-
siders feelings largely invalid and relatively unimportant.
Most of us can remember crying when we felt hurt as children
and hearing well-intentioned adults say "it's not so bad" or
"you're okay." Some of us were even told outright that we
shouldn't have been feeling what we were feeling at all.

In all fairness, we need to acknowledge that our parents' intention when they unknowingly discounted our
emotions was to make us feel better. Our parents didn't plot
to repress our expression of emotions. They were only
doing what they thought was best.

However, as children faced with adults telling us that
everything's okay when it isn't or that we don't have a good
enough reason to feel what we feel, we easily learned to
repress our emotions. We had no room to express our feelings because it seemed that those around us wanted us to

quickly get over them; and as our repressing became more automatic, we grew more unaware of what we were feeling. Unfortunately, feelings that we're unaware of can affect us even more than those we know about. The more we repress, the more we overreact to similar situations. I can remember boys in junior high school who would punch somebody for looking at them the wrong way. In retrospect, I can guess that they were having serious problems at home with no other outlet for their subsequent hurt and anger.

On the other hand, some of us learn to repress our feelings in reaction to adults who overreacted to them. When we skinned our knees bicycling, our parents got hysterical and decided that it wasn't safe for us to ride a bike. Eventually, we learned to hide our feelings to avoid all the hubbub.

In an environment where people consistently discount feelings or overreact to them, we learn that we're not free just to have and express our feelings. We bottle up our feelings until we can't hold them in anymore, and then we displace them by overreacting. We come home and kick the dog or yell at somebody.

How sharing our feelings enhances our relationships

Regaining our ability to know what we're feeling and to freely express our feelings to those we love greatly enhances our relationships. When we share what we're feeling, we're letting others into our lives, and they no longer need to guess what we're experiencing. When Jill shared her feelings with her husband, he felt closer to her and no longer had to wonder why she had been withdrawing from him. Also, the more we share our feelings directly, the less we displace our feelings. Consequently, our friends and family can witness and validate our feelings without dreading our next angry outburst.

Sharing our feelings helps us move through them quickly and easily. When we share our feelings without judgment, we feel okay to feel what we feel. This validation of our feelings empowers us to move through them and leave our past bad feelings behind us. When Jill and I validated her feelings, she began to remember that she loved her husband; she remembered that their relationship was important enough for her to risk sharing her feelings with him.

When we express our feelings directly, others get to know how they're affecting us and they are then free to choose how to respond. I recently consulted with the founders of a small company. They'd just brought a new person on board whom they experienced as being whiny and complaining. They hesitated to confront her because they generally felt very pleased with her work and feared offending her and hurting her feelings. I first acknowledged them for being sensitive to her, knowing that in business settings we're often insensitive to how others feel. Together, we determined that it was her tone of voice and focus on problems rather than solutions that elicited their reaction. They were then able to talk to her about her behavior in a respectful and inclusive way. They even had some helpful suggestions for her. As it turned out, this wasn't the first time that she'd gotten this feedback, and she knew that she had a problem. However, no one had offered her specific suggestions about changing before. Subsequently, she was able to use these suggestions to change, and ultimately she felt more like a part of the team.

Sharing our feelings in a respectful way helps us clarify misunderstandings. Many times our words and actions have intentions that are different from how others receive them, and a lack of feedback about how we are affecting others can lead to much bigger problems. For example, we can easily hurt or offend someone and not know it when they fail to tell us. I can remember as a college student visiting a girlfriend's home and getting in trouble with her parents because I came to breakfast in a tee shirt. In their family, coming to a meal without fully dressing was considered disrespectful. We could have avoided the whole problem if someone had told me ahead of time because putting on a shirt was no big deal for me. Instead nobody told me, and her parents subsequently developed a poor opinion of me without my knowing why.

I'm not saying that we need to respond to everyone's feelings, but that knowing how others feel can give us the choice to respond. Sometimes, all we need to do is understand how others are reacting to us and accept their feelings.

Here's an example of how sharing feelings can enhance a relationship. Recently, I told my wife that I felt like an outsider in our family. My daughters were getting older and my work was taking me away more often than I might like. It seemed that she and my daughters had a life that didn't include me, and I felt left out. After moving past our guilt feelings and blame, we were able to discuss whether there was any basis in real events for my feelings or if I just needed to have my feelings witnessed and validated. We decided that there really was a basis for my feeling like an outsider. She and the girls were doing a lot of things without me, and I was slowly drifting outside the family circle. Eventually, we were able to generate two possible solutions: we could collaborate more when dealing with the girls, and I could spend more time with them including being with the girls when my wife wasn't around. So sharing my feelings provided the opportunity for us to do something to change the drift in our relationships, and things have gotten a lot better since we made these changes.

If I had not expressed my feelings, my unexpressed feelings would have continued to grow under the surface. Eventually, I probably would have displaced my feelings by overreacting to something else or by just becoming generally grumpy and irritable. After a time, I would have predictably withdrawn even more from the family because I felt so bad being around them, and the girls and my wife would have distanced themselves from me because I was being "such a pain."

Maintaining healthy and alive relationships requires that we become aware of our feelings and sharing them. Sharing our feelings helps us avoid misunderstandings and gives us the opportunity to be responsive to each other, bringing us closer and creating the intimacy that we all crave.

How we learned to keep our thoughts to ourselves

Early in our lives, many of us learned that our opinions weren't important or wanted. Adults were often too busy or distracted to ask us what we thought, and they came from a culture where "children should be seen and not heard." Treating children as unimportant has its roots in thousands of years when a high percentage of children failed to live past the age of five because of infectious disease, poor sanitation and malnutrition. Why invest emotionally in someone who wasn't likely to be around for very long? Many cultures didn't even give permanent names to children until they survived these early years. Not until recently, perhaps the last 100 years or so, have enough children survived their early years to generate more emotional investment. But we're only beginning to learn how to treat children with the respect that they deserve.

Most of us have some childhood experience of adults not honoring what we thought, and some of us were even ridiculed or punished when we spoke up. Consequently, we learned to keep our opinions to ourselves, not letting others know what we were thinking. Some of us still don't.

Some of us, however, learned more subtle ways to keep our thoughts to ourselves. I can remember making observations and having the adults around me get quiet or tell me that was not really the way things were. When we talked about things that were outside the accepted realm of common understanding, we invariably received responses that let us know that we should have kept these thoughts to ourselves. The young boy who points out that the emperor has no clothes is usually told to keep his mouth shut. When we varied from the norm, we were quickly led back, and if we saw things in a slightly different way, we learned to keep it to ourselves.

We also learned to avoid expressing ourselves in order to avoid conflict and hurting others' feelings. In an environment that doesn't tolerate differences in opinion or conflict, we quickly learn to avoid conflict by keeping quiet. When we mistakenly learn that we are responsible for others' feelings, we become careful about what we say, fearing that if we say the wrong thing, someone will be hurt.

In one way or another most of us learned to not share our thoughts with others. Men, especially, have had few models for sharing and talking about things. We just don't talk very much. I can remember finding out many of my father's opinions of me only from my mother after his death.

Many of us learned to talk with each other without really being self-revealing in any way. We easily talk about the weather or our favorite baseball team but almost never about what is really important to us like our hopes and dreams. We create lives filled with acquaintance, instead of intimacy.

There's nothing wrong with acquaintance and we don't need to be intimate with everyone; however, it's important that we share our closely held thoughts with those we love. Talking about the weather or the latest news is interesting but doesn't create much intimacy.

The importance of sharing our thoughts with each other

Just like sharing feelings, sharing our thoughts lets others into our lives. Sharing our opinions helps us understand and tolerate each other. The other day, we were watching the movie "Field of Dreams" on television when my wife noticed that I felt deeply moved by the last scene, the one where Kevin Costner gets the chance to play catch with his father. Later, we talked about what I was feeling, about my relationship with my father and how I missed having the opportunity to share some of the important things in my life with him because he'd died soon after my first daughter was born. She asked me some thoughtful questions, and I told her some things about myself that I'd never shared with her. In a way, talking with her helped me gain a better understanding of my own feelings about being a father and my strong desire for a good relationship with my daughters. This is another advantage to sharing our thoughts with each other. Somehow in the process of sharing, we get to uncover deeper parts of ourselves and gain more self-understanding. Later, she told me that she now had a better understanding of some of my reactions. Subsequently, she's felt more compassion for me and been more patient with me as well.

Sharing with each other helps us to serve each other. A few days ago, my wife heard me describe this book in detail to my daughter's teacher. She later called to tell me that I'd never really explained the whole book to her, sharing only bits and pieces. I had no idea that I hadn't shared it all with her. She said that hearing about the whole vision of my book gave her a sense that it could really make a difference for people who read it. Consequently, she's been much more willing to support me and make any sacrifices that we might have to make to help me finish the book on schedule.

When we share our thoughts, we don't have to guess what's going on for each other. We know what we each want and what's important to us, and we can more easily help each other create fulfilling lives together. Knowing that my wife would like to be with her father on his birthday, I can make sure I'm available to watch the children that weekend. Sharing with each other saves us from having to mind-read each other. It saves us from the projections that we naturally make when we don't know what others are really thinking and from the problems our inaccurate projections often create.

Dumping grounds into oases

When we aren't honest and straight with each other about what we feel and think, not sharing what's really going on for us, our relationships become dumping grounds. When we don't talk about what's bothering us, we displace our feelings by overreacting and being miserable. We use our relationships to dump our bad feelings, making our loved ones the victims of our circumstances.

On the other hand, when we share our thoughts and feelings, our relationships become oases where we can be nourished and replenished. Sharing our feelings and thoughts with our loved ones helps them support us by letting us know that our feelings are okay and that they value what we think. Our relationships become a place where we can safely and comfortably express ourselves.

When we share our thoughts and feelings, we gain a better understanding of each other. That helps us be more tolerant and accepting of each other, creating an environment in which we can more easily change and grow into who we are capable of being. Nourished and replenished by this environment of acceptance, we feel better equipped to go out into the world. We know that whatever happens we have a place where we can relax and just be ourselves. Our relationships have truly become oases where we can find respite and emotional nourishment. We have a place where we know that there are others who love and support us just the way we are.

Being honest and straightforward allows us to take down the barriers that we've built between us and begin to create true intimacy. This provides much of the raw material for our forgiving by letting us know what there is to forgive. When we're honest and straightforward we reveal what we need to work through and ultimately forgive, increasing intimacy in our relationships. Thus, we propel our relationships into the present where we can express our love and caring for each other.

The Advantages of Sharing Our Thoughts and Feelings

1. We avoid guessing games — others get to know what we are really thinking and feeling.

2. Others are free to choose how to respond to us.

3. We stop acting out our feelings unfairly.

4. We move through our feelings more quickly.

5. We get to clear up misunderstandings.

6. We can better serve each other.

Tool #8—Sharing Yourself

Sharing creates intimacy by letting others into our lives Sharing reveals our humanness to each other and gives us the opportunity to be compassionate and forgiving. It helps us avoid the tragedy of arriving at the end of our lives feeling that no one ever really knew us.

Sometimes, though, we withhold things that we need to share in our relationships, often because we want to spare someone's hurt feelings. Other times we withhold in order to preserve the image that others have of us. And more than we like to admit, we can withhold to avoid dealing with the potential damage precipitated by our mistakes.

Withholding means not sharing our news, what we've done and what's happened to us that might affect our relationships. My daughter deciding not to tell her best friend that she's changing schools because she doesn't want to make her feel bad is a good example of withholding. Another example is someone not telling his family about a serious illness. The most dramatic withholding in a marriage or partnership, of course, is hiding an affair.

In this chapter, I'll explain how being fully straight, honest and forthcoming with each other is the best way to ensure a truly intimate relationship. You'll also learn how withholding can be a surefire way to strangle and kill a healthy, living relationship.

How we learned to hide the news

Most of us learned to withhold early in life. Maybe we came home from school all excited about something, and our parents ignored us or our older siblings told us we were either "stupid" or "being a baby" to be excited about something so unimportant. Or maybe we discovered that admitting our mistakes only got us punished, so we learned to hide them. Later, as teenagers, we teased each other about almost everything. We can all remember times when others responded to our "news" with insensitivity and, at times, even cruelty. No wonder we learned to be careful about what we revealed to others.

We also come from a culture that believes in protecting others from their hurt feelings, that it's even our duty to spare others' feelings. We learned to spend a lot of our time and energy managing our relationships by deciding what to reveal and what to withhold with the supposedly good intention of sparing others' feelings. This was our model for how to be caring in a relationship and, because we care about those we love, we learned to protect them in this way.

The cost of withholding

We can justify withholding by believing that "what they don't know won't hurt them." But, in fact, what they don't know *can* hurt them. When we withhold from others we diminish intimacy by blocking our connection with them. Whatever we withhold is always there between us, like a cloudy screen that keeps us from experiencing the clear love that we have for each other. Our relationships become defined by what we're withholding from each other instead of what we have to share. It's probable that if my daughter withholds our decision to move from her best friend, my daughter will begin feeling uncomfortable whenever she's around her. Eventually, she'll begin to distance herself from her friend. Then not knowing what happened, because all minds abhor a vacuum, her friend will likely think that she's done something wrong herself. Their connection to each other will begin to fray, and eventually they will grow apart, never knowing what really happened.

Lying or withholding something requires that we manage our relationships instead of being in them. More and more energy goes into covering up what we're withholding because it's always present and we can't get away from it. Eventually, being together becomes our stimulus for remembering what we're withholding and feeling bad about not being straight with someone we care about. Every time my daughter is with her friend, she'll think about what she hasn't told her. And if she tries to stop thinking about it, she can't because it's like trying to not think about elephants. The more we try to ignore it, the more it's there.

We can get a real education about how withholding creates problems in relationships by watching sitcoms on TV. Actually, sitcoms have historically based their comedy on laughing at the problems that withholding creates. "I Love Lucy" is a great example. In almost every episode, the plot revolves around something Lucy withholds from Ricky in order to avoid his disapproval. Then in the course of the show, all kinds of funny complications result from her withholding. We watch Lucy create bigger and bigger lies, getting herself in all kinds of jams where she can display her comic genius. Things get more and more complicated until, in a hilarious climax, it all collapses like a house of cards. Ricky gets to be stern with Lucy, then forgive her, and they live happily ever after. Much like real life, except for the living happily ever after part.

Unfortunately, in real life we rarely share our withheld secrets, creating bigger and bigger walls between us, never suspecting that we have created them ourselves. Eventually, we become alienated, feeling distant from those we love without knowing how it happened. An interesting fact is that in real life Lucy and Ricky's marriage didn't last, apparently because of Ricky's infidelity.

Withholding creates disparity in our relationships. Protecting others from knowledge of our problems is a statement that we consider ourselves more capable than they are to deal with problems. This is appropriate in parental or guardian relationships, but not in equal partnerships. When we withhold in order to protect others from their feelings, we're stating that they're less capable of dealing with life's difficulties. We're putting ourselves in the superior position of deciding for others what they can't handle, holding ourselves as more able to deal with the difficulties that naturally arise in life. Under the guise of helping them, we're really keeping others from maturing and growing. They never get to handle those difficult situations that are the raw material for developing maturity, confidence and the skill to deal with life.

When we withhold from others in order to protect or spare them, we create even bigger problems. The wife who doesn't tell her husband about the problems that their children are having at school is treating him as someone who's less capable than she is to deal with these problems. Being left out of the loop leaves no opportunity for him to learn to become a more capable parent or for her to learn that he already is. When we protect others, we create extremely fragile relationships that haven't tested and proven our ability to face problems and work through them together. We treat our relationships as fragile objects that we need to protect, never learning how resilient we can be when we're committed to communicating and having things work for everyone.

Knowing what to share in guardian relationships

In a parental or other guardian relationship, protecting our children or wards from emotional situations is appropriate and even necessary. Children don't need exposure to all the brutalities of life, and they don't need to deal with complex situations that they're not mature enough to understand. My wife and I don't need to involve our daughters in every problem we have with each other. Children can often take things to heart that aren't very important or significant to adults. Until they're older, they don't need to know about our financial concerns or our intimacy issues. Children are concrete thinkers, often making mountains out of mole-hills. I can remember thinking my father was gone forever when he left angrily during an argument with my mother. I wasn't old enough or mature enough to know that he just had to blow off some steam and that he'd be back.

However, even as parents and guardians we must remember that withholding isn't always the best way to protect and care for others. For example, when Peter came to me for therapy, complaining of not being able to sustain an intimate relationship, we found the source of his prob-lem in certain emotionally traumatic events in his childhood. The most important was when his loving grand-mother died when he was six. She'd often taken care of Peter, and when she died unexpectedly, his parents didn't let him attend the funeral. Maybe they thought he was too young to understand, or maybe they were just too upset to think clearly. But, they never explained to him what had happened, and Peter, understandably, felt confused and lost. Like magic, one of the most important people in his life was here one day and gone the next. Not knowing why his grandmother had apparently abandoned him, he filled the void by imagining, as children often do, that he was responsible for her leaving. Feeling ashamed, he never talked about this to anyone, and eventually his unresolved guilt had a significant effect on his self-esteem. He grew to feel unworthy of intimacy and unconsciously believed that if he got close to people, they would leave. The six year-old inside him, who still felt guilty about grandma leaving, wouldn't let him get close to anyone ever again.

Deciding what to share with children is an important and sometimes difficult responsibility. We need to balance protecting them from growing up too early with letting them gradually learn how to deal with life's challenges. Peter's parents needed to talk with him about what had happened to his grandmother and they probably should have let him attend the funeral so that he could get some completion with her. He would understand as much as he could, and instead of being isolated during this hard time, he would have been with those who loved him and could care for him. This would have helped him understand and deal with his grandmother's death.

Deciding what needs to be shared

Deciding what to share in a relationship is difficult. We have so many thoughts and feelings that, if we shared them all, we would have time for nothing else. When they were young, my daughters gave me a verbal play-by play of everything they were doing. "I'm washing my hands now. I'm washing the dolly's hands now." Fortunately, they grew out of this before I stopped thinking it was cute. Adults who share all their thoughts aren't nearly so cute. It's hard to tell what's important, and after awhile, we just stop listening. We all need to learn how to discriminate, sharing those things that are important for us to share and leaving room for just being and playing together.

On the other hand, some of us need to learn to share more. We tend to be too closemouthed and don't share things that are important to our relationships. One test for whether to share something is if our withholding affects our behavior. When I don't feel free to be myself in a relationship, then I know there's something that I need to share, even if all I share is that I'm not feeling free to be myself. Often, however, because there's something else going on for me, I need to turn my attention inside and find out what it is. When something is affecting how we're behaving, we need to identify it and then share it. Anything that gets in the way of our freely being ourselves begs to be shared.

My style when I withhold something is to withdraw and shut down. Others may become impatient and critical or talk about trivial things. Each of us needs to identify how we generally behave when we're withholding something so we can become more easily aware of it when we are and then get our relationships back on track.

Important decisions also beg sharing. The wife who withheld from her husband that their children were doing poorly in school needed to include her husband in the process of deciding what to do. Our relationships become stronger when we work together to solve our problems. We even need to include our children in family decisions as long as we don't burden them with adult responsibilities. Though discovering this line between including our children in family decisions and giving them too much responsibility can prove difficult, we must include them as much as possible.

We don't need to share all of the trivial details of life, even though sharing them can foster intimacy. When I react emotionally to something and my emotions truly pass without affecting me further, I can just let it go. Something is truly insignificant when not sharing it doesn't make a difference in a relationship. However, whenever we feel compelled to withhold something, it is significant because if it were truly insignificant we wouldn't feel compelled to withhold it.

Many decisions need only one person's input. I'm the gardener in the family. My wife has no interest in gardening even though she appreciates the flowers and vegetables that I grow. I don't need to consult with her about what fertilizer to use or what annuals to plant this year because she's fine with any choice that I make. She's content to let me handle it. There are other things that I'm content to let her handle. This kind of complementary sharing of some responsibilities can foster a strong sense of trust in our relationships. However, we do need to continually check whether we are not sharing things that we should be. I know, for example, that before I want to cut down some trees to expand the garden, I need to talk it over with my wife.

Infidelity

People in committed, monogamous relationships who have sex outside of their relationship usually withhold this from their partners. I can understand why they do. They rightfully think that sharing it might threaten or even end their relationship. What they don't realize is that not sharing is also likely to end their relationship. Even if they stay together, their relationship will never be the same because their infidelity will always be between them whenever they're together. Many relationships dissolve because of this kind of withholding.

When we withhold something of this magnitude, it inevitably affects the relationship. One partner has gone outside the relationship to fulfill a need that they need to address within the relationship. Whenever they're together, it will affect how they are with each other. The cheating partner may be withdrawn, angry or even disingenuously over-attentive. No matter what the behavioral response, an event like this will always affect the relationship in a serious way.

I don't believe those who claim they can sufficiently compartmentalize their lives so that their indiscretions don't affect how they respond to their partners. In the very least, there will always be a limit to their intimacy because there is something that they can't share.

I'm not moralizing about non-monogamous relationships here. Those who make agreements in their relationships that include outside intimate relationships need only to make sure that they're living within their agreements. I am, however, stressing the importance of being straight and honest in a relationship. Intimacy in any relationship depends strongly on there being no significant withholding in the relationship.

When We Need to Share

1 When we don't feel free to be ourselves.
2. When we have decisions to make that effect others.
3. When we feel misunderstood.
4. When we feel distant or alienated from others.

How to communicate
our mistakes

Sharing our mistakes is difficult at best. How we communicate our mistakes can influence the response we get even more than the mistake itself. When we need to share something that is hard to understand or even painful for someone, how we communicate is very important. Before communicating we must get in touch with our commitment to our relationships. This is, after all, why we're sharing. It's our commitment to having intimate, healthy relationships that is the source of our desire to clear things up. After getting in touch with our commitment, we can begin our communication by restating our commitment. If I forgot to plan for my wife's birthday, I need to begin by telling her that I care deeply about her and our relationship. I then need to state that I'm committed to being open

· 153 ·

and honest with her and that I'm willing to do whatever it takes to have the relationship work for both of us.

Whether others believe that we're being truthful about our stated commitment can depend on how badly we've hurt them. Not planning something special for my wife's birthday might not be a big deal for her, but making an important decision about our living situation without consulting her probably would. In this instance, I can understand her questioning my commitment. However, I still need to state my commitment, whether she believes me or not, because when she eventually begins to move through her hurt, I can continue to be strong in my stated commitment and behave in ways that support what I say — to walk my talk. Of course, walking my talk needs to include consulting with her before important decisions in the future. "Sorry" can wear thin when it doesn't lead to change.

Whenever we confess something, it's essential that we not defend or justify our behavior. Defending and justifying our behavior dilutes taking responsibility for what we've done. Justifying our mistakes eliminates responsibility because we're saying that we're at the mercy of our circumstances. When I apologize for a mistake with a lot of excuses, I'm saying that the circumstances did it, not me. We can always find good reasons for mistakes. If circumstances made me do it then, if the circumstances return, they doom me to do it again. Using circumstances to excuse my behavior only weakens my commitment to be different and pretty much guarantees that I won't change.

In contrast, when we take full responsibility for our actions, trust returns more easily. If we are responsible for what we did, then we can be responsible for changing. When we take full responsibility, others can trust us to be more thoughtful and responsible in the future.

When we share that we've violated an agreement in a relationship, others will surely react. Even though it's not news to us, it's news to them. We've had time to deal with our feelings, but because we've been withholding, they haven't. They will likely feel angry and hurt. We can best heal our relationships by being absolutely willing to witness their expression of their feelings and any reaction short of physical violence. This is possibly one of the most difficult things to do in a relationship, to listen to someone's anger and hurt in response to our actions without getting defensive or angry back. If my wife feels more hurt and angry than I anticipated, I need to listen to what she has to say without defending myself. Being committed to loving intimacy, I must stay present to her expression without making it about me by defending myself. I've already admitted that I messed up. If I get defensive or withdraw, I'm demonstrating that I have less interest in her well-being than in my own comfort.

The simple formula is to stay close if we want to be close, especially if things are bad. Of course, it's also important to honor a request for space; but we never need to use the request for space as a reason to flee the scene and abandon our commitment to healing our relationships. We need to give space but continue to be available, hanging in there for as long as it takes.

How to Communicate a Mistake

1. State your commitment to your relationship.

2. Be responsible — do not defend or justify your behavior.

3. Be willing to witness others' reactions to your sharing without withdrawing.

By facing crises and working through them together, we gain the confidence in our relationships to trust our ability to handle our problems. By moving through difficulties together, we learn to trust that we can work through any problems that arise. Ultimately, we reach a place where we believe that there's nothing that we can't handle together. Our commitment to being open and sharing becomes so strong that we become truly responsible for our actions. Subsequently, we can use the energy we free up from chronically withholding and managing our relationships to become more conscious of our thoughts, feelings and actions. Eventually, we become more intentional about doing and saying those things that support our commitments. Being more conscious and intentional, we will ultimately make fewer mistakes. We begin to form a snowball of positive regard and caring that grows, gaining size and momentum forever as it rolls down the hill that is our commitment to being fully alive and engaged in our relationships.

By sharing what we think and feel with each other, we create more dynamic, healthy relationships. Thus, our commitment to communicate and be vulnerable with each other is the key to bringing our relationships back to life.

Tool #9—Nurturing Your Partnerships

When Fred called me to arrange an appointment for him and his wife, Karen, he told me that she'd recently asked for a divorce. He said that he didn't understand why she was so unhappy in their relationship; all he knew was that he'd been a good provider who didn't drink or beat her. They'd been married for 15 years, since their early twenties, and had two girls, ages thirteen and seven.

At our first meeting, Karen said that she'd been a stay-at-home mother, and that now she was ready to begin working outside the home. She was glad to have stayed home with the children, but with both girls in school she wanted to get out in the world more. However, she wasn't sure whether she wanted to go right to work or back to school for a graduate degree.

When I asked her why she wanted to leave Fred, she said that Fred was absolutely opposed to her working. He responded that he made enough money to support their family and couldn't understand why she wasn't content being his wife and the mother of their children. After some probing, Karen revealed that when she'd worked after they first married, Fred had been extremely jealous, accusing her of having an affair with her boss. Whenever she went out without him, Fred would grill her about where she'd been and what she'd been doing as soon as she got home. Eventually, she grew weary of arguing every time that she wanted to go out with her girlfriends, and she stopped seeing them. She thought of leaving Fred back then; however, she became pregnant with their first daughter and decided to stay.

When I asked her why she wanted to leave now, Karen said that she was tired of fighting about her desire to go to work. When I suggested that this was a problem we could probably work out, she admitted that this wasn't her only reason for leaving. She revealed that Jessie, their 13 year old, was becoming a teenager with her own ideas and desires. Jessie and Fred had apparently been getting into huge arguments about what she wore to school and who her friends were. Recently, Jessie had begun to stay out past her curfew, getting hostile when they questioned her about where she'd been. As a teenager, Karen had rebelled against her own controlling father by becoming involved with drugs and alcohol and being sexually promiscuous. She saw the danger signs in Jessie and knew that something had to change.

I knew that saving this marriage would take a lot of work. Both Karen and Fred came from dysfunctional families. Fred's father was an alcoholic and beat his mother. I started by telling them that, considering the families they'd come from, they'd done a terrific job with their girls, and now they'd come to me to learn how to evolve their marriage and their parenting so that they could continue to do a terrific job.

The process of relating

Much of the difficulty we have in relating to each other comes from treating our relationships as possessions. Historically, men learned to perceive their wives and children as chattel, a possession with a certain value. You weren't married so much as you had a wife. Your children were valuable for what they could produce through work or in the way of a dowry. Even though we think that we've come a long way from these archaic values, we still tend to treat our relationships as possessions. We are often more interested in having relationships than in caring for them

However, our relationships are not things — they are processes of relating. Consequently, the tools and concepts that we developed to deal with relationships as possessions don't work with the process of relating. Even if we're not in as much trouble as Fred and Karen, we can all benefit from learning to treat our relationships as the processes they are.

The difference between processes and possessions

Once we realize that relationships are processes and not possessions, we can discover that all these ways we learned to deal with our relationships as possessions no longer serve us. They can even be damaging to our relationships. Our challenge is learning a new set of skills for successfully relating to each other. But in order to decide what tools we need, we must first understand the differences between processes and possessions.

Processes are alive and always changing, requiring our ongoing and frequent attention and care. Like all living things, relationships that we don't care for get sick and die. In contrast, possessions aren't alive; they are dead things. Because possessions are dead, our primary, and often only, concern is keeping them safe so that we don't lose or damage them. So as long as we consider our relationships to be possessions, we try to keep them safe at the cost of their aliveness. When relationships are possessions, keeping a relationship becomes more important than the quality of our relating. Treating our relationships like dead possessions, we've concerned ourselves with preserving our relationships instead of caring for them. Let me share an example of treating a living thing as if it were dead.

Several years ago we got a puppy from the animal shelter. We named her Lucy, and ever since she has been an important part of our family. As many of you already know, caring for a dog takes time and attention. Because Lucy is alive, we need to feed her, groom her, train her and love her. If we stopped caring for her in any of these ways she would suffer and maybe even get sick and die. In contrast, if we considered her to be merely a possession, our primary concern would be having her and not losing her. Maybe we could fence her in, but this would not protect us from losing her to disease. With this in mind, a great way to keep our possession, Lucy, safe would be to take her to the taxidermist, get her stuffed and put her out in her pen. When people visit we could point out to the pen at our beautiful dog and proudly say, "She's a great dog. She never gives us any trouble, and we never have to worry about her."

Traditionally, men and women have learned distinctly different ways to treat their families as possessions. Men have primarily been providers. We've learned the importance of providing for our families at the expense of relating to family members. We go out of the home and work long hours so that our family members can have the things that they need and want. Women are primarily caretakers. They have learned to take care of their families in the same way that dairy farmers take care of their cows, doing all the daily tasks that provide for a healthy physical environment. Their major concern is physical well-being, often at the expense of intimacy. Just as we men can provide for our families without experiencing intimacy, women can take care of physical needs without experiencing true intimacy.

Living relationships are at risk

We can best keep our relationships alive by realizing, that like all living things, they are at risk. The risk for a living relationship is killing it, so we need to do whatever it takes to keep our relationships alive. You will find that it's worth the effort because healthy relationships are alive, evolving and changing along with the individuals in the relationship. Ultimately, they enhance the growth and personal evolution of all the individuals in the relationship.

In contrast, dead relationships aren't at risk. They are zombies, the living dead. You can't kill them because they're already dead. Dead relationships don't evolve because they fail to adapt to the natural changes that we all go through. Things stay the same, with little room for individual growth and change.

When we recognize that our living relationships are at risk, we become motivated to change any behaviors and attitudes that could kill our relationships, things like taking others for granted and not sharing our feelings and thoughts. Knowing that without active care our relationships will stagnate and die of inertia, we become empowered to take active responsibility for attending to and caring for our relationships.

The importance of being vulnerable

The best way to keep our relationships at risk and alive is taking the personal risk of being vulnerable. This means sharing things we might normally keep to ourselves, thoughts and feelings that we fear others will reject and judge as silly, stupid, foolish, or immature.

Sharing is courageous. When we share our deepest and most intimate thoughts and feelings, we open ourselves to possible rejection, becoming vulnerable to the responses that we get. If we've been rejected in the past, we can be so afraid of revealing ourselves that we even fail to tell those we love that we love them because we're terrified that they won't love us back.

Learning to be vulnerable is absolutely essential to building healthy relationships. Only by sharing can we let others get close enough to know us and accept us as we really are. In a sense, being vulnerable is an act of trust. We trust others to care enough about us to accept and appreciate whatever we reveal to them, without judging us. We share ourselves, hoping that others will love us in spite of what we think and feel, that they will love us for who we are.

When I share my fears with my wife, she gets to see more than just my competence and confidence; she gets to experience my human imperfections. Thus, I become more approachable and available. Also, sharing my fears and concerns makes it easier for her to share her fears and concerns with me. We get to be vulnerable with each other, and our fears become less important. Fears are like spiders in a closet. They're always a lot bigger when they live only in our imagination. When we open the door and really look at them, they're smaller than we imagined.

Karen and Fred's relationship is a perfect example of what happens when partners withhold from each other. Karen didn't share her concerns about Jessie with Fred, because she saw him as rejecting and judgmental. When Karen didn't share her fears with Fred along the way, he had no clue that there was a problem in their relationship.

Subsequently he was shocked when she revealed her unhappiness with their marriage.

As we worked together, Karen and Fred realized that they needed to share their past with each other. He didn't know about her rebellion against her father, and she didn't know how much his father's alcoholism and abuse had affected him. Before we discussed it in therapy, Fred hadn't even realized that he was reacting to his feelings of instability as a child by being controlling as an adult. Both of them were constantly reacting to their past experience, letting their childhood experiences dictate their behavior as adults. Consequently, they were both too afraid to be vulnerable enough to reveal themselves and risk rejection. So in order for them to benefit from therapy we needed to begin by making it safe enough for them to be vulnerable with each other. Once we established a sense of emotional safety, we could rededicate all the energy they'd been using to hide their past and present fears to working on their relationship in the present.

When we share ourselves with each other, we free all the energy that we'd been using to hide. All our fear of rejection dissolves, and we receive the gift of energy that comes with knowing that it's okay to just be ourselves. Eventually, we also discover that we have loving allies who will help us with the problems and challenges in our lives.

Nurturing and caring for our relationships

Because all living things require nurturing care, we need to notice what begs our attention. For example, we feed our dogs more in the fall when they're too thin to stay warm in the coming winter, and we feed them less in the spring when the hot summer months are approaching. As living things, our relationships also need nurturing. But in order to succeed at nurturing our relationships, we need a good barometer that can tell us how we're doing, indicating whether our relationship skies are clear or cloudy, whether we can expect fair weather or a storm is brewing.

If Fred had been paying attention, he would have noticed that there was a problem. At our first session, Karen revealed that she'd been withdrawing from Fred for more than a year. She said that they didn't talk much anymore and that their sex life had become almost nonexistent. But Fred didn't notice that things had changed because he wasn't paying attention.

Along with a good barometer, we need a good compass. Because healthy relationships aren't just alive, they also have direction that we call meaning and purpose. Relationships are journeys that are about both discovery and destination. Therefore, we need a good compass for determining whether our relationship is on course, taking us where we want to go together and individually.

Historically, the barometer we've used when evaluating the health of our relationships has been the answer to the question "Is the relationship working?" Often, we ask this question when we're deciding whether to stay in a relationship or leave. But this question doesn't work very well for keeping a relationship healthy and alive because it treats them as entities in and of themselves. It separates the health of our relationships from our participation in them, as if whether our relationships are working is somehow unrelated to how we act in them. It treats them as objects or things that are static, unchanging, and independent from us. This question and attitude are right for deciding whether a jacket that I'm thinking of buying fits and is the right color and style for me. Does this jacket work for me? If it does, I buy it. If it doesn't, I go to the next store.

Our relationships are living processes that depend on our participation in them. So the question we need to ask must consider whether we're doing what will make our relationships work as living, growing entities. If we decide that we are, we can continue to do what we've been doing until we notice that it's no longer working. For example, after our first daughter was born and my wife was busy nursing and attending to our daughter, she mostly needed me to support her by taking care of our day to day needs. This freed her to give our daughter the kind of attention that we believed a newborn could best get from her mother. My wife did not need a great deal of physical attention from me. Instead, when she put the baby down, she needed a break from being touched. Other women may have different needs, but this is what she needed. Later, as our daughter grew and began to take more of her own physical space, my wife needed me to be more physical with her. She now welcomed the hugs that used to feel stifling and crowding to her as an expression of our love and caring for each other.

When we care for our living relationships, the question "Is the relationship working?" can be replaced by the question "How will we make our relationship work?" Instead of focusing on whether our relationships are working, this question helps us think about what we need to do now and in the future to keep them working. It allows us to consider what we can do to make sure that we're all being served in our relationships. What will it take for us to stay on course?

Defining the course of a relationship

Before we can decide whether we're on course, we need to map out our course by defining our goals, what each of us wants to achieve through our living together. In most relationships we never openly discuss our goals and needs. Since the mind abhors a vacuum, if we don't discuss things openly, we'll jump to all kinds of conclusions that might not be what we really want.

This kind of mind-reading or conjuring can turn a relationship into a tragicomedy where two people spend their entire lives working towards goals each believes the other wants but which neither really wants. Without openly discussing their goals, a couple might toil at their jobs to save enough money to obtain a certain degree of financial security, only to discover too late that they both really wanted to spend more time together, enjoying each other and their children. By the time they realize that they would have been more than willing to give up some future financial security for this precious time together, it's too late.

Another tragedy occurs when we limit what we do to what others taught us to do. We base our lives on our childhood experiences, without thinking about whether what's important to us as adults is different from what was important to our parents. We live our lives on automatic pilot, eventually awakening to the realization that we relived our parents' lives without ever considering what we wanted.

Don't wait. You need to sit down now and discuss what you want from your lives together. Families need to include everyone in this discussion, including children, by meeting together and talking about what's important to you. You need to discuss your goals for the future, your dreams and your aspirations. You need to discover what goals you share and how you differ, and then talk about how you can best achieve your goals and fulfill all your needs together. Then by examining your present course, you can determine whether your course is aligned with your goals and needs. If not, you can forgive yourselves for being off course and determine what changes you can make to accommodate everyone's needs. Then put these changes into action. It's never too late to create the life you truly want. It may or may not be the life your parents wanted for you, but you'll be taking an active role in designing your lives. You'll move beyond passively living lives based on your unconscious early learning and old assumptions about how life should be.

When we take an active role in designing our lives, we discover that we have much more energy for doing whatever will move us closer to our goals. When we're on course, we can accomplish even the most difficult tasks as we move forward in achieving our lives' fulfillment. Problems become challenges and opportunities for discovering how capable we are. Mistakes become learning opportunities that shape our ability to succeed in the future.

Setting goals and needs in our relationships is also a living process. We must be sensitive to whether our present goals are still what we want. Things change and so do people. When Fred and Karen's girls grew older, they needed to expand their life to include her working outside the home. We need to keep our finger on the pulse of our relationships to determine if our goals continue to meet our needs and wants. I suspect the needs of my family will change as our daughters grow into teenagers and adults. By sitting down periodically and reexamining our goals we ensure that we are being intentional about where we're heading, so that we can make wise choices that will take us where we want to go. We want to be able to look back on our lives and see that we at least attempted to create what we really wanted, and maybe even that we succeeded.

After a lot of work together transforming how they were reacting to their own upbringing, including uncovering their unresolved emotions and expressing them, Fred and Karen were able to talk freely with each other about what they wanted their lives together to look like. Fred was able to share that he was insecure about Karen's love for him and realized that he had tried to control her in order to be safe. Karen was able to see that she failed to express her needs to Fred because she feared being rejected and actually created what she feared, a husband who imposed his needs on her. Happily, their sharing created room for them to begin to design how their lives could be. They realized that they didn't want a life based on reacting to their unhappy past. Fred began to see that in fifteen years he'd learned that Karen was someone he could trust. Karen began to realize that the more she shared with Fred, the safer he felt and the less controlling he needed to be. He began to support her in looking for work while she began to share herself more, and together they talked more about their children.

Getting where we want to go

Having a good idea of our goals gives us parameters for deciding what to do to reach our goals, which is our next challenge. If we rely solely on our own sense of things, we fail to use our most valuable resources, the people around us. The best way to make good decisions is working together in relationships because collaborating creates better solutions than acting independently. Plus we get the added bonus of helping us feel more connected to each other.

Along with active collaboration, close observation can help us make sure that what we're doing supports those we love. I've been with my wife long enough and observed her closely enough to have a good sense of when she might be having a problem. If she replies to my telling her that I'm going to do some writing now by saying "OK" with a certain strained tone of voice, I suspect that all is not well with her. The trap that most people fall into at this point is to interpret the tone of voice. If I did, I might decide that she doesn't want me to write now, but I might be wrong. She might only have a toothache. When I suspect that something is wrong, I need to check it out with her. I might ask her if she doesn't want me to write, only to discover that she's worried about something at work and my writing now is fine because she needs some time alone to think about it. We can arrange a time to talk later. Another possibility is that she does have a problem with my writing now; so asking her about it unmasks our conflict, and we can decide together how to resolve it. In either case, checking out the meaning of my observation helps me fulfill the goals and needs of our relationship. My advice is to notice when something is "off" without jumping to conclusions. It's always best to check out what someone is really feeling and thinking rather than making it up yourself.

The paradox of safety

The more we're concerned with preserving our relationships, the more we feel the threat of losing them. Conversely, when we treat our relationships as living processes, keeping them at risk by being vulnerable with each other, the more they become arenas for our full self-expression, and we feel safer in them.

If relationships were dead things, then keeping a relationship safe would mean preserving it by creating physical safety. However, relationships are alive and do not require physical safety. In a living relationship, only the individuals require both physical and emotional safety.

Physical safety is easier to clearly define than emotional safety. Physical safety means respecting each other's physical space, not striking each other or even touching each other in ways that we don't clearly desire and invite.

Emotional safety, however, is more complex because it's paradoxical in nature. We feel safe in our relationships when we make ourselves vulnerable to each other through intimate sharing. When my wife shares herself with me, I feel freer to open up to her. My sharing makes it easier for her to open up to me in turn. This free expression of emotions and opinions makes us feel safe in our relationships. When we're free to express ourselves within clear boundaries, we can more easily witness and honor each others' expression. Thus, we create an upward spiral in which we learn to trust each other more and more. The more we share with each other and the more we experience our ability to resolve conflicts, the more we know that we're safe to be ourselves in our relationships, trusting our ability to handle whatever problems arise.

Without intimate sharing in their relationship, both Fred and Karen found it hard to feel safe. When they began to talk about their feelings and thoughts with each other, including their personal histories, they began to see the other as vulnerable as well. Consequently, they both became more willing to open up themselves. Fred was no longer like Karen's father who never opened up to her, and

Karen was no longer unpredictable like Fred's father. They both felt safer knowing what the other was experiencing.

The dysfunctional family

Unfortunately, many of us learned to repress our emotions and opinions because we didn't feel safe enough to express ourselves in our families. Whenever we expressed our opinions or emotions, we were ignored or told to keep it to ourselves. There was certainly no permission to express uncomfortable emotions or opinions that differed too much from the norm.

Because the adults in these families experience free expression as a threat, they try to limit it by controlling what others do and say. One way of controlling others is to become autocratic and dictatorial. Another way is to withdraw without revealing yourself because you fear being judged. Fred tried to control Karen and their daughters by being autocratic, while Karen sought control by withdrawing. Both these responses interrupt healthy sharing and initiate downward emotional spirals in which there is gradually less information available. Everyone is guessing what is going on with the other, and the idea of opening up and sharing becomes more and more threatening.

In dysfunctional families, there are many secrets and those who reveal those secrets are scorned and "excommunicated." There is absolutely no permission for family members to communicate their feelings about any abuse that has occurred, whether sexual, physical or emotional. Unfortunately, without this communication, those who are responsible can't admit to what they've done and get the help they need to heal and change their behavior. Without revealing the abuse that has occurred in a family, there's no opportunity for forgiving, and without forgiving there's little chance for healing and creating new ways of relating. When abuse remains secret, the love that's always been there, the love that made the abuse so painful in the first place, also remains secret, hidden underneath the unexpressed hurt and anger.

This is why I don't support the blanket rejection of abusive parents by their victims. I do support rejecting their parents' abusive behavior, while forgiving them for this unacceptable behavior. At the same time, it's also important that I honor people who have experienced abuse by not pushing them to forgive before they're ready. However, if I support them in rejecting their parents fully and with finality, they're prolonging and forwarding the same dysfunctional patterns that we're trying to leave behind. They are "excommunicating" their parents in the very same way that their parents might have "excommunicated" them for revealing the family secrets.

To create function in the space of dysfunction, the children need to acknowledge what occurred, even if their parents can't. Then through separating who their parents are from what they did, the now grown children can forgive them, empowering themselves to move on in their lives with a new family tradition of openness and forgiving. Forgiving their parents, however, does not require that they get closer to their parents. That's another decision. Forgiving does, however, recognize, express and acknowledge the love that all children have for even the most abusive parents. It allows them to make a more up to date decision about what kind of relationship to have now. If parents are still abusive, children can love them from enough distance to feel and be safe.

Eventually with my help, Karen was able to forgive her father for what he'd done. She was able to start a new relationship with him, becoming surprised to discover that he was no longer as recalcitrant and rigid as he once was. Because he had mellowed over the years, they were able to have a better relationship than they'd ever had.

The functional relationship

In healthy functional families and relationships, everyone is free to express what they feel and think. Individuals feel safe to express themselves, and everyone feels accepted and honored. I'm not painting a rosy picture of relationships without conflicts. All relationships have conflicts. But a healthy environment in which we all listen and honor each others' expression helps us hang in there. When there's a conflict or disagreement, we persist until we've worked things out, even if we have to agree to disagree.

The best way to create emotional safety in our relationships is by honoring everyone's expression unconditionally. That doesn't mean agreeing with what everyone says, but witnessing what they communicate, really listening, so that everyone feels heard. Fred has to hear how Karen feels about his rigidity, and Karen needs to hear how Fred feels threatened by her desire to get a job outside the home. This unconditional listening creates a safe environment in which communication can flow freely. Subsequently, the energy that we might have spent mind-reading and managing others in dysfunctional relationships can go towards helping achieve the goals of the relationship and fulfilling everyone's needs and desires. Once Fred and Karen have really heard each other, they can begin to create a relationship they really want to be in.

Replacing control with flexibility

Functioning well in living relationships requires that we be flexible and sensitive, responding to changing needs and engaging in an ongoing communication process that sets a direction for our relationships. We need to be sensitive enough to recognize the need to alter our course when our goals have changed or if we recognize that our present course is not heading where we want to go. Then we must be flexible enough to change.

Being flexible is contrary to trying to control our relationships because we're afraid of losing them. When we want control, we attempt to limit things so that there are fewer variables to handle. Fred doesn't like change because it makes him feel out of control. In contrast to control, being flexible includes accepting the complex nature of life and relationships and using our perception and sensitivity to adjust and adapt to the changes that occur naturally in all relationships. If Fred becomes flexible enough, change will no longer be something to fear, but merely something to handle.

Being flexible helps us trust that we can always do something or communicate in a way that will make a difference. We trust that no matter what happens we can figure out some way to make things work. It gives us a sense of personal power, not a power over others, but the power to act in cooperation with others.

Flexibility distinguishes influence from control. Influence differs from control by being cooperative in nature. Influence requires that we enroll others in cooperatively creating what we'd like to have together. Everyone becomes involved and everyone wins. When my wife wants something from me, she needs to enroll me by speaking to me openly and honestly. My role is to be open and willing to listen, consider her ideas and be enrolled. In contrast to this, the basis for control is limiting options and variables and therefore, requires that we limit the influence and power of others. Others' power is just another set of variables that if eliminated will allow us to have more control. Control creates more and more static rigidity that eventually squeezes the air and life out of our relationships.

Control is a powerful weapon that we can use to kill our relationships through our fear of losing them. If I want to be in control, I will kill my relationships because I can't stand the suspense of knowing that I could lose them. In contrast, influence requires that we engage in the cooperative process of making our relationships work for everyone — this is the lifeblood of our relationships, empowering us to honor everyone's expression, wishes and contribution. This is love in action.

How to Keep Relationships Alive

1. Be vulnerable — share your feelings and opinions.

2. Continually ask, "How will we make our relationship work now?"

3. Discuss your goals and needs together.

4. Update your goals when needed.

5. When you think there might be a problem, check it out.

Tool #10—Expressing Conditional and Unconditional Love

Raymond originally came to me for help with panic attacks. After we relieved his panic disorder, he decided to continue in therapy to get help with some other concerns. Now 36, he had been married once for a few years in his twenties and been in three serious relationships since, each lasting less than a year. When I asked what kind of relationship he would like to have, he described a very romantic connection, without conflict, one in which he and his partner did everything together. Probing further, I discovered that all his relationships started to "sour" early on. He described how every time, after a few months, he started to fall out of love, realizing that his partner was not whom he thought she was. It seemed to me that when the romance and infatuation in his relationships faded, he "fell out of love."

Raymond described himself as a perfectionist. Making mistakes was intolerable to him. He found it hard to resolve having "made the wrong choice" so many times when picking partners, and he was hesitant and anxious about trying again. When he was in situations where he could meet women, he was too nervous to talk to them. Interestingly, he had his first panic attack when a friend "dragged" him to a gathering for single professionals. I knew that Raymond had to first learn some things about making mistakes and then about love in order to feel relaxed enough to meet someone.

Saying we love someone can mean many different things. We can love our children, love a husband, love a friend, love a car and love our country. Sometimes, when we say that we love, we mean little more than like. Love can also mean a great deal more. We can even love others without liking them. I have noticed, however, that relationships in which people like as well as love each other often succeed. We can spend a great deal of time and energy just tolerating others when we don't like them, time and energy that we could spend simply enjoying them. We've all witnessed relationships in which the partners appear to be fonder of each other when they're apart. These relationships define the cliché, "Absence makes the heart grow fonder."

The experience of love

Determining exactly what love means is challenging because each of us experiences many different forms of love. But no matter what our experience, each form of love occurs for us as a particular set of feelings. For example, infatuation for a new lover might feel like a combination of excitement, expectation and attraction. The love we feel for our children might include caring, pride, a sense of protection and a deep feeling of connection. Every experience of love then is a unique and different set of feelings.

Though we seem to treat love as an abstract concept, our actual experience of each of these different forms of love occurs as a particular and specific set of bodily sensations. We feel these feelings in our bodies. We might feel the excitement of a new romance as a fluttering sensation in our stomachs or chills down our spines, while the comfort of a long-standing relationship might give us a warm feeling in our bellies. How we experience a particular feeling doesn't matter as much as knowing what we're feeling by being in touch with our bodily sensations.

Finally, our experience of love is always subjective. The bodily sensations that I identify as excitement may be the same or different from how you feel excitement in your body. And how I define a particular set of feelings may be different from how you define them. The bodily sensations that are excitement and attraction for me might be fear and loathing for someone else. In the same way, a feeling of comfort might be an important component of love for one person and not for another.

Evolving love in partnerships

In healthy partnerships, love moves through developmental stages. Some feelings may last from one stage into another, but usually our whole package of feelings that we call love grows bigger and deeper through the addition of new feelings.

When I first met my wife, I felt feelings of physical attraction and liked her personality. Soon I was experiencing the excitement that let me know I felt infatuated with her. Gradually, over time, my love for her evolved to include a certain feeling of comfort and familiarity. The excitement had lessened, thank God, but the attraction was still there, and my love felt deeper in some way. When we married, my love developed a dimension that included a sense of commitment and loyalty that it didn't have before. I also felt a sense of sharing that gave me an experience of solidity over time, greatly deepening my love for her. When our first daughter was born, I experienced a feeling of gratitude towards her and a much deeper feeling of connection.

My love began to include the feeling that we could participate in creating a miracle together. With subsequent
experiences, my love for her continues to grow and deep-
en. Even our difficult times together have added to my
experience of love for her. Getting through our problems
helps me trust that we can make it through some hard
times and have our caring and love survive and grow.

Limiting our experience of love

Sometimes we limit our experience of love by confusing
love with a particular form that love takes at one stage in a
relationship. We might think that love is those feelings of
excitement and sexual attraction when we first meet someone. Unfortunately, if we think that one particular form of
love is all that love can be, we fall out of love when our
feelings predictably change. Because Raymond confuses
love with the infatuation he feels at the beginning of his
relationships, he "falls out of love" when the infatuation
fades. So love never lasts for him and he falls out of love
easily, failing to ever create a long-term relationship.

If we feel attached to a particular form that love takes,
we fall out of love when our love naturally shifts form.
Confusing the totality of love with one of its forms guarantees that love won't last. When people say that they've
fallen out of love, they are revealing that they have lost
touch with the particular feelings that they defined as love.
When we attach love to a particular set of feelings, as soon
as the feelings change, love fades.

Changing love

Recognizing that love changes and evolves in the course of any relationship sustains our love. Changing feelings no longer mean falling out of love. We can relax and allow our feelings to shift without becoming alarmed that our love feels differently than it used to feel. As his infatuation fades, Raymond can begin to notice that there is the possibility for a deeper love with room for all the imperfections that both he and his partner have. Accepting that infatuation can pass while love remains, he can begin to learn about a love based in commitment, support and a shared life. Romance doesn't have to fade, but he can realize that there are many ways to relate to each other in a committed relationship, with romance being one of them. Sometimesthe frequency of sex is not as important as the connection experienced during sex.

When we accept that love naturally changes, we can choose to shape the form that our love takes at any time. After our oldest daughter began to grow, and my wife and I found ourselves faced with each other more, we brought back the fire into our romantic relationship by doing things that made us feel special and attractive. Being attentive and really listening to each other helped reawaken the romance in our relationship. Of course, whenever we do something to change the form that our love takes, we need to notice whether what we do gets the response we want. Buying flowers might be a sign of love and caring to one person, but a sign that you are trying to buy love to someone else.

Conditional and unconditional love

Though love can take many different forms, all forms of love fall into one of two categories. All love is either conditional or unconditional. Our love is conditional when it depends on some circumstance being met. We love someone because of how they look, because of their personality or because of our history with them. When our love has a reason, it's conditional. The physical attraction I feel for my wife is a conditional form of love. I feel attracted to her *because* of the way she looks to me.

Unconditional love doesn't change when conditions change. It is the love we feel in spite of conditions. It is unchanging and invariable. Consequently, it is more elusive and harder to define. It is the love I feel for my wife that doesn't vary with our aging and changing relationship.

Learning to love unconditionally

Our relationships are our classrooms for learning how to love unconditionally. They are our vehicles for evolving conditional love into unconditional love because, as our love grows, our love becomes less and less dependent on circumstance. When we first meet, our love depends on certain conditions being met, like physical appearance and personality. We feel drawn to others because of the way they look or because they are friendly and compassionate.

As our love grows, it becomes less and less dependent on conditions. We no longer base our love on how someone behaves or looks. We begin to experience a love that transcends change and never wavers. Our unconditional love doesn't replace our conditional love so much as we allow our love to grow and a new form evolves that is so much brighter that it outshines our conditional love.

Conditional love serves as our vehicle for learning about unconditional love by placing us in close proximity to other human beings. When we fall in love with someone, we naturally want to be close to them. We want to enjoy the good feelings we get from being with them. However, after infatuation wears off, and we begin to perceive them as more than our projections, we become more aware of all the ways they express themselves in the world. We get to witness not only things we perceive as good, but the bad as well. When this happens, we begin to judge them. We discover that they are too thin or too heavy, too serious or too flaky, too quiet or too talkative. We might not like the way they treat their friends or the way they treat us. There are an infinite number of human characteristics and behaviors we can and will judge.

Our judging others, however, is not their problem. It's our problem because we're not able to accept them as they are. So when we begin to judge those we love, our challenge becomes expanding our conditional love into an unconditional love that can transcend our petty judgments and empower us to learn how to love and accept them as they are. Because all human beings are imperfect, we need to love unconditionally in order to overcome our judgment of each other.

On the other hand, if we continue to judge others and expect them to change so that we can more easily love them, we become victims of our conditional love, a love that we can never fully satisfy. "If she would only be more (fill in the blank) then we could stay together." In contrast, when we allow ourselves to stay close in our relationships in spite of our judgments, we begin to realize that our judging, and not their imperfection, is the problem. Thus owning our judging as our own shortcoming, we create space for unconditional love.

How unconditional love leads to change

One of the most interesting aspects of the relationship between judging and unconditional loving is that we're least likely to change when we feel judged and most likely to change in positive ways when we feel loved unconditionally. When we feel judged we begin to feel unloved, inadequate and bad about ourselves. We become defensive and dig in our heels, resisting any changes. Feeling bad about ourselves in this way makes it difficult to find the inner resources we need to change. Even if we want to change, we just aren't able to find the strength for it.

In contrast, we tend to feel good about ourselves when we feel loved unconditionally. Consequently, we become more aware that we're not what we do or how we look, and we become more open to change. Feeling good about ourselves inspires us to change in order to express more fully these good feelings about ourselves.

As Raymond and I worked together, we discovered that his perfectionism, his intolerance for making mistakes, was born in his childhood experiences with his mother. He experienced her as critical and unloving, feeling that he could never do enough to please her. Now as an adult, he played this critical role for himself by never being satisfied with his own performance. The result is that he hesitates to take the risk of failing because his sense of self depends on his success. As we began to free his sense of self from his performance, he was able to take some of the risks that used to terrify him.

When I judge my wife, I make her responsible for the well-being of our relationship. She has to change for me to love her. I am cloaking her and our relationship in the negativity of my judgments. "Our relationship would be fine if you would only change."

In contrast, when I love her unconditionally, I project love into her. My love resonates with the place inside her where she already feels truly loved. My love breathes life into her strong sense of self, so that she can freely love from a place of strength, feeling loved herself. Our relationship then becomes the vehicle for the free expression of our love for each other.

The best thing I can do to help my wife improve herself is to fully express to her that I love her just the way she is. She doesn't have to change anything for me. Consequently, any changes that she does make will be self motivated and be a true reflection of her inner self. This doesn't mean that I can't make requests about her behavior, but I need to understand that any change I request is not a judgment of her, but merely something I want. My request has nothing to do with her value as a human being or how she's being as a wife and mother. My requests are about me. Loving her unconditionally, I give up the game of being responsible for her personal evolution, and I take responsibility for my true job in our relationship, loving her unconditionally.

Conditional and unconditional love working together

Unconditional love is like the full moon coming out from behind a dark cloud and outshining the stars of our conditional love. The stars are still there, but don't add much light when the moon is out. They helped light the way before the moon emerged, but their light pales in comparison. However, even though they are no longer necessary for lighting our way, they are still beautiful. The mistake that some make is to ignore the stars when the moon is out. When our love achieves the illumination that unconditional love provides, our conditional love will be able to enhance our relationships by creating a personal expression for our love. Sex, for example, can be great when it's an expression without the pressure of being the only thing that keeps love alive. Conditional love shapes our love as a personal expression that reflects our individuality and unique natures.

Neither conditional nor unconditional love is more important than the other. Healthy relationships need both. Each, however, serves different functions. Unconditional love allows us to experience the joy that love can be when it is unchanging and eternal. It is the love that is always present, providing us with the direct experience of perfect love and acceptance.

Conditional love allows us to make the choices that life requires us to make. We have the right to choose from what distance to love someone, and conditional love is what allows us to make this choice. I want to be distant from someone who abuses me and closer to someone who is considerate and kind. I want to be closer to someone whom I find interesting and stimulating and more distant from someone with whom I have little in common. I can love the abusive person unconditionally and safely from a distance because unconditional love is not dependent on conditions and does not fade when conditions change. Proximity is just another condition.

We each have our own set of criteria to determine how close we want to be to somebody. Our criteria may be personality traits, commonality of interests, cultural background or any of an infinite number of things. We need these criteria because without personal preferences the more we love the more we would be doomed to want to be close to everyone.

Unconditional love allows us to be fully in love while conditional love allows us to have a life. We can choose with whom we wish to share our lives without losing touch with the love that we have for all people and all things. Unfortunately, we sometimes experience difficulty in realizing unconditional love for those we dislike. This happens when we fail to distinguish conditional love from unconditional love. We can clear up this confusion by realizing that conditional love depends on an object, another thing or person, while unconditional love is self-contained. Unconditional love comes from within us and is solely dependent on our realization of the love within us and not what others do. My unconditional love for my wife does not depend on what she does but whether I am open to my own inner connection to love.

Unconditional love comes from inside us. It is the expression of our true self. In this sense, it is not so much something that we can achieve, like romantic love, as something that we can realize. It is an opening that occurs in spite of us. The beauty of relationship and conditional love is that conditional love can over time begin to awaken our experience of unconditional love within us. Conditional love is our normal human experience that most resonates with unconditional love.

We can empower our conditional love to give rise to our unconditional love by first clearly distinguishing between these two forms of love. We then need to give up our attachment to any particular form that our conditional love takes. Our willingness to let our love change form frees us from our attachment to particular conditions. We shift our attention from looking outside ourselves when deciding whether to love someone or not to looking within and discovering that love is already within us. This practice of shifting our attention within helps us notice our unconditional love as it awakens within us. As our unconditional love awakens, we can enjoy the feelings that arise, and others will begin to notice changes in us. Our petty jealousies and envy will fade away, and we will gain compassion and kindness toward others that can serve as a beacon for their growing love. In return others' love will serve as a beacon for us.

Working through our fears

When unconditional love begins to awaken in us, we begin to feel any fear we still have about not being loved. Unconditional love is the beacon that illuminates us and provides us with the opportunity to deal with fears that we haven't yet resolved.

When our fears arise, we can either panic while emotionally shutting back down or accept that opening to love includes working through our fears that limit our ability to be loving and fully self-expressed. Our fears arise only when we fail to love. Therefore, working through our fears and learning to love are really two aspects of one process. Our love grows as we resolve our fears and our fears subside as our love grows.

Those who think that all is love and light are onto something, but can sometimes fail to see that their fears and personal demons are part of this love and light. If all is love, then even fear is a part of love. If we fail to deal with our fears then we're just fooling ourselves about how much we truly love. We're making our unconditional love dependent on not having too many fears, thus making our unconditional love conditional.

Unconditional love is paradoxical in that it accepts all things, including not loving. One of the most powerful ways to awaken unconditional love is to practice loving yourself in spite of being too afraid to sustain this love. Bringing the light of love directly into the dark cave of our fears illuminates them so that we can begin to work through them. In this way we begin to resolve our fears and move through them by embracing them without either believing them or avoiding them.

Our personal preferences help us choose with whom we wish to share our lives and what kind of life to have together. Our conditional love gives us the freedom to shape and direct our lives.

Being free to choose includes being fully responsible for the choices we make. There is no absolute, purely external authority that tells us what to do. When we're free, even responding to some external authority is a choice. When I'm free, I can choose to have a life that my mother doesn't approve of, and I'm also free to choose a life that she would approve of.

Because love includes being free and responsible for our choices, another fear that arises with growing love is our fear of making mistakes. Being fully responsible for our choices includes being responsible for our mistakes. Therefore, as we take more responsibility for our lives, we naturally begin to feel any fear we have of making mistakes. When Raymond begins to step out into the world, engaging in finding a partner, all his fear of failing arises. His challenge is to keep moving forward while working through his fears.

Admitting our fears and sharing them with others reduces their importance and potency. It is an act that says that we're willing to reveal ourselves and be vulnerable, and we're saying that on some level we know that we're not our fears, that we just have fears. When Raymond shared his fears with me and found that I didn't recoil in shock and disgust, his fears lost some power over him. By sharing our fears, we discover the compassion that others have for us. Every time someone responds compassionately to our revelation of our fears, we strengthen our understanding that our fears are fears that most of us share in common. The measure of the courage it takes to be fully responsible for our lives and thus powerful and effective is not the absence of fear, but who we are in the face of our fears.

As we become more aware of our fears and reveal them to others, we will witness love coming alive for us. Others will respond to us with compassion and our own inner love will begin to awaken and illuminate our true loving and compassionate nature. This love and compassion will outshine our fears and allow us to let go of any identification we still have with them. They will no longer run our lives by unconsciously making our decisions and choices.

Instead, we will be able to make choices from the place that is love inside us, where we love all others and even ourselves.

When we're no longer afraid, we're free to love each other as we are. We become lights that shine on everyone's unique and individual expression. We love each other for who we are, supporting our freedom to explore who we are and how to fully express ourselves. We all feel fully honored and respected as we use our love to light the way for each other.

Working through our fears gives rise to the freedom to love each other as we are. This and other freedoms are an important part of any healthy relationship. However, being free in our relationships requires understanding commitment in a new way.

Love in Relationships

1. We experience many different forms of love.
2. Any form of love is a set of feelings that we feel in our bodies.
3. In partnerships, love changes form over time.
4. Relationships need both conditional and unconditional love.
5. Conditional love draws us to relationships so that we can learn unconditional love.
6. Feeling judged hinders change; feeling loved unconditionally facilitates change.
7. Recognizing and resolving our fears facilitates love; awakening love dissolves fear.

Tool #11—Making True Commitments

Jane, 43, had always "done the right thing." She met her husband, Steve, at college, and after they married she worked for several years as an office manager. Soon, however, she decided to stop working and stay home to raise their two children. Meanwhile, Steve advanced in his career in a large telecommunications company, where he was now a director making a very good living. Steve was very conservative, however, Jane had begun to realize that her own opinions and viewpoints were different than she'd always believed them to be.

Jane had not pursued her own career, but she had become active in the community by doing volunteer work for various charitable organizations. Recently, she became involved with animal rights activists, feeling more passion than she'd felt in a long time in her life. To her surprise, she discovered that she had a great talent for enlisting support for her causes. She particularly had a great deal of success getting those with seemingly closed minds to listen to a different viewpoint.

Jane was feeling confused and upset when she first came to see me. Her organization had just offered her an important job in Washington as a lobbyist. She knew that this was her dream come true and she was seriously thinking of taking it, but there were real problems. For she and Steve to stay together, he would have to relocate and try to find new work in the D.C. area. This idea of disrupting her family went against everything she'd learned about women in families — that women were obligated to subject their wishes to those of their husbands and children. She recognized that it would be hard for her children to leave their friends and for Steve to give up his hope of further advancement in his company. He was adamantly opposed to her taking the job. He didn't even want to continue discussing such a "ridiculous" idea. Jane had begun to wonder whether she shouldn't take the job anyway. I began by letting her know that whatever decision she made, it was okay to want something for herself.

Freedom means having choice in our lives. When our behavior is shaped by our feelings of obligation and duty, we have almost no choice in our lives and little freedom. When I work to provide for my family because it's my obligation as a husband and father, I don't feel free to choose to not work because society will judge me harshly if I don't fulfill my obligation and duty.

As I stated earlier, we are presently evolving from relationships based in obligation and duty to relationships based in choice and freedom. One concern that arises when we use choice and freedom as a basis for our relationships is that we will have nothing to ensure that we stay in our relationships without feeling obliged to. This concern is valid, however, only when we stay in our relationships because we feel obligated to fulfill our duty.

The problems with obligation and duty

Those who stay in relationships because of obligation and duty find it hard to even imagine that someone would actually choose to be in a relationship. They think like this because relationships based in obligation and duty do not nurture and sustain people very well. If we feel obligated to stay, there's no need to enroll us to stay. No one in his or her right mind would actually choose to stay in such a relationship without feeling obligated to. Feeling obligated is the only thing that keeps them from leaving.

When obligation and duty rule our relationships we feel controlled by some outside force. Others have predetermined what we do, and we have little say in it. Without choice we feel powerless, angry and resentful. Our relationships are prisons with choices occurring only within a narrow predetermined band of possibilities. Our well-being is secondary to the well-being and survival of our relationships, and over time we lose our sense of purpose and our feeling of aliveness fades.

For the first forty years of her life, Jane did what others expected her to do. She was a good wife and mother, experiences that she would not give up. But when this new possibility arose, she experienced a great deal of resistance from others and from inside herself. When she walked in my door, she felt worried and concerned, but she also felt very angry and resentful. She had never questioned her relationship before, but now nothing seemed certain. For the first time she faced really knowing that she could choose to stay in her relationship with Steve instead of staying because that was what a "good" wife did.

Choosing a relationship is hard work and requires a great deal of personal responsibility. It's no wonder that anyone in a relationship based in obligation and duty might find it difficult to imagine that someone might actually choose to be in a relationship when they don't feel obliged to. The question then is "when we don't feel obligated to, how do we actually choose to be in a relationship?"

Commitment

As personal freedom grows, commitment replaces obligation and duty as the basis for relationships. Understanding
the difference between commitment and obligation and
duty will empower us to choose our relationships because
of our personal commitment to them.

The most important difference between commitment,
and obligation and duty is that while commitment comes
from inside us, obligation and duty originate outside us.
Commitment relies on our personal decision and choice.
We define our commitments for ourselves, and we are
responsible for fulfilling them. On the other hand, others
define our obligation and we allow them to impose it upon
us through subtle demonstration and learning. We often
don't even know that we're living our lives from obligation
and duty because there's never any discussion of other possibilities. How we've been told our lives should be seems
like the only possibility. We fulfill our obligation and duty
because that's what we're supposed to do, and if we don't
there's something wrong with us. In contrast, commitment
is free. We're free to choose our commitments, and we're
free to choose how we fulfill these commitments.

Choosing

Commitment gives us more choice and freedom because no
particular choice is inherently better than any other. We
each decide for ourselves what to choose because outside
authority can no longer tell us what we should do to fulfill
our obligation and duty. Every life choice is a good one
because we have chosen it.

Only with respect to reaching certain specific goals are
some choices better than others. For example, if I have the

goal to have children and live with them and their mother, then marriage is a good way to move in the direction of fulfilling my goal. This choice to marry, however, is better than the choice to stay single only when I have goals that I can better meet through marriage. With different goals, staying single might be the "better" choice for me.

Each of us is responsible for deciding whether our choices will be effective or not. I decide whether my choice to be a husband and father is the right choice for me. However, if in the middle of my choice to be a husband and a father I decide that it's not right for me, I must deal with the circumstance that I have created by being responsible to my choice. Being a husband and father is a choice that has ramifications over time that I must respect. Being responsible to my wife and children because I have freely chosen to be, I need to deal with the ramifications of my change of mind. Any changes I want to make must consider everyone's needs.

Living our lives from personal choice instead of a sense of obligation and duty brings a different mood and energy to our lives. Many of us have known someone who returned to school after dropping out at a younger age. Initially, they dropped out of school because school was something that they *had* to do. They had little reason to be in school, so when they felt that they could, they dropped out. Education was not yet a useful thing for them. Later, however, after they realized that they could actually benefit from an education, they returned to school. This time, though, they knew why they ought to be in school, and they had chosen to go back. More often than not, these born-again students feel highly motivated, their performance improves and they usually finish school. Any teacher knows that these older students who have chosen to return to school are often the best in the class. This is a good example of the difference in mood and energy between externally motivated behavior and self-motivated behavior.

Similarly, when I take responsibility for choosing to marry and have a family, I bring a positive energy that supports my choice. I am fully behind my choice, and I can be effective and influential in co-creating my family in a way that nurtures and supports all of us.

I'm not saying that we shouldn't do things that are traditionally our obligation and duty. Rebelling is not free choice either because we feel compelled to do anything but what we feel obligated to do. In a sense, when we rebel we feel obligated to *not* fulfill our obligation and duty. When we truly have choice we are also free to choose those things that have traditionally been our obligation and duty. My choosing alone doesn't energize my marriage because they are very similar to the choices that my father made. However, my ownership of these choices does. I am free to choose what I have chosen or free to choose something else.

Commitment and responsibility

Every commitment we make is personal because all our commitments are essentially with ourselves. Even when we make a commitment to someone else, we are choosing it. We, not others, are responsible for deciding whether we are successfully fulfilling our commitments. When I tell my wife that I'm willing to commit to having children and raising them in a way that we believe is in their best interest, I'm making this commitment with myself. If I later have a problem with the way we're raising the kids, I don't blame my wife and claim that she was the one who wanted children in the first place. Instead, I take responsibility for my choosing by discussing with my wife the problems I'm having with my commitment.

Something very similar to this happened when I decided to write this book. In order to create time to write I needed to cut back on my practice and thus decrease our income for a while. This was at odds with my commitment to be the primary provider for our family. At first, I got angry with my wife because she wasn't working more or earning more money. Instead, I needed to approach her and talk to her about what I wanted to do. Eventually, even though I felt a little crazy at the time, I was able to share my feelings with her, and we agreed to make some changes and commit to handling any hardship that arose. Actually, she was much more relaxed about the situation and experienced my commitment as being looser than I did.

Choosing our commitments makes us responsible for them. We are responsible for fulfilling our commitments and, if they don't work out, for dealing with how our failure to honor our commitments affects others and ourselves. We have no inherent obligation to fulfill our commitments, however, we need to know that what we do affects others. We must be willing to work out any problems that arise from our actions.

This is true freedom. When we own the choices we make by taking responsibility for our commitments, we are responsible when things work out and when they don't. Unfortunately, this is our biggest problem with freedom. Most of us find it difficult to admit our mistakes and failure. Our culture relies on externalizing responsibility when things go wrong, so that we don't have to bear the weight of our mistakes. "It's not my fault. I was just doing what I was supposed to do." The extreme of this kind of thinking is the "I was just following orders" that we heard so much after World War II when the Holocaust came to light. A more recent externalization of responsibility is the TV evangelist who blames the devil for not reaching his donation goal.

When we base our relationships on freedom of choice and personal responsibility, commitment becomes the vehicle for creating relationships that last. We now need to define the nature of personal commitment in relationships. Exactly what do we commit to when we want our relationships to be alive and healthy?

Creating healthy commitments

Creating and maintaining healthy relationships requires two specific commitments: a commitment to our partner's well-being and a commitment to communicating. Our relationships remain healthy only when our commitment to their lasting is less important than our commitment to communicating and the well-being of our partner. I knew that if there were going to be any hope for Jane and Steve, they had to start communicating again, and Steve needed to accept that Jane's needs and wishes deserved at least serious consideration. I do not believe in staying in a relationship that is not nurturing and supportive of both partners. Fortunately, however, being committed to another's well-being paradoxically creates relationships that are worth keeping.

In contrast, when our primary commitment is to a relationship lasting, we can create a relationship that is not nurturing and supportive of one or both partners. When Steve became scared about their relationship lasting, he tried to control Jane by dismissing her idea and refusing to talk about it. Needing to preserve his relationship at all costs just made him controlling and insensitive.

Why control based relationships don't work

When our primary commitment is to preserving our relationships as they are, we'll behave in ways that restrict and limit our relationships in order to keep them safe. Steve attempts to limit Jane by refusing to even consider the possibility of changing the course of their lives together. His focus was on the survival of their relationship rather than toward using their relationship as a vehicle to support their growing and evolving together.

When our primary concern is keeping our relationships, we focus on their survival by trying to control everything. Wanting things to stay the same, we use control to keep them from changing. Our partners become just another thing we need to control. After all, if things change, you might leave. So in order to keep our relationships safe we focus on managing and controlling our partner's behavior. Steve tries to control Jane by telling her that she can't consider her "ridiculous" opportunity.

When control is our method, fear is our mood, and our primary feeling is jealousy. We fear that our partners may become dissatisfied with our relationships and go somewhere else to get their needs met. Ultimately, our jealousy can even become a self-fulfilling prophecy. If we think about infidelity long enough, it begins to become real for us. We then increasingly question our partners, and if we don't control our fears, eventually we begin to falsely accuse them. Our partners feel abused, and the possibility of breaking up increases dramatically. Because they don't feel honored and nurtured in our relationships, they may eventually seek comfort with others and live out our fears. This is the extreme example of what happens when our primary concern is the survival of our relationships. However, even when things don't get this bad, when our main focus is the survival of our relationships, our partner's well-being becomes less important than staying the same.

When Steve hears of Jane's offer, he becomes scared for their relationship. However, instead of trying to understand Jane's needs and consider her wishes, he tries to shut her down by refusing to speak with her. Predictably, she feels incredibly unsupported by him and begins to wonder whether she should stay in their marriage.

The paradox of relating is that the more we try to control our relationships, the more likely we will lose them. The more controlling we are, the less nurturing, supportive and trusting we become. If I try to control my wife's behavior, so that I can feel safe in knowing that she will stay with me, I fail to attend to her needs. My only concern is that she stays where I can keep an eye on her. This is at the least emotionally abusive, and in relationships where physical abuse is prevalent the physical abuse goes hand in hand with the husband's attempt to control the wife's behavior, often going as far as restricting the wife to the home.

The desire to control is rooted in insecurity. We fear that if we don't personally make things happen the way we want them to, they won't work out. Our fear, however, is incompatible with trusting that we have the ability to do what it takes to maintain healthy relationships. There is no room for trust and faith in fearful relationships

Relationships based in trust and faith

In contrast to relationships based in fear are those based in trust. This is an active not a passive trust because we trust our ability, together with our partners to handle whatever problems arise. We trust that we genuinely care for each other enough to do what it takes to support each other. By focusing on our partners' well-being, we're saying that we honor them so much that if it were ever in their best interests to leave, we would support even this. Paradoxically, our truly supportive attitude increases their desire to stay. Who would want to leave someone who really has his or her best interests at heart?

If Steve would show his love for Jane by honestly supporting her in considering her opportunity, she would stop wondering if she should stay in their marriage. She would want to make sure that any solution they arrived at included preserving their marriage. A decision might still be difficult, but if they continue to communicate and stand strong in their resolve to do what is best for everyone, their relationship will grow stronger regardless of what decision they make.

When we trust that we are truly concerned with each other's well-being, we don't have to devote as much energy to taking care of ourselves. Taking care of each other, we grow closer and more connected. Also, when I feel that my personal needs are being taken care of, my definition of my personal needs begins to expand, eventually growing enough to include my partner's well-being as well. My wife's well-being becomes actually part of and not separate from my own well-being. The ultimate extension of this phenomenon is the Buddhist tradition of the Bodhisattva who is committed to the enlightenment of all individuals. These enlightened beings continue to incarnate as long as there remains one individual who is not yet enlightened. Our mutual trust creates a positive spiral in which what goes around comes around in a way that works for everyone.

To summarize, when our commitment in our relationships is to the well-being of our partners we increase the possibility that our relationships will last. We create a mood of faith and trust, honoring each other through our commitment to each other's well-being. We feel honored and cared for, and therefore have more energy and attention for honoring and caring for each other.

Communicating

The second commitment that ensures the well-being of our relationships is a commitment to communicate. As I stated before, good communication includes both speaking and listening. Helping our partners fulfill their needs and desires in our relationships requires listening well enough to discover what they are. We too often think that we serve someone by doing for them what *we* think will help them — better to listen and discover what they think will help. My wife sometimes wants me to give her space to handle something herself. As my natural bent is to have my fingers in everything, this can be a difficult request for me to honor, but I do my best.

When our needs are considered, honored and, if at all possible, fulfilled, we are more likely to freely express what we need and want. This free flow of information enables us to trust that together we can discuss and handle anything that arises. Problems that previously seemed insurmountable become opportunities for creative solutions. If Steve and Jane both felt that their needs are important in their relationship, they would be much more empowered to handle their new problem. They could work together, communicate freely along with their children, consider their options and take the time they need to arrive at a good decision.

Handling problems

When we create relationships based in our commitment to the well-being of our partners and to full, honest communication, it's easier to handle any problems that arise. Our problems don't threaten our relationships because our mood is faith and trust rather than fear. Our problems are just a normal part of our relationships. With our commitment to each other's well-being, our relationships become strong enough to deal with any problems that arise.

Living within our strong commitments helps us accept the problems that naturally arise whenever a relationship evolves from one level of development to another. What best serves us at one level of functioning is not necessarily the best thing for another level. Early in their marriage, it served both Jane and Steve for him to work outside the home and for her to stay at home with their children. But as the children grew older, this changed. The training wheels that helped my daughter when she first began to ride her two wheeler became a hindrance when she began to develop her sense of balance and wanted to take those turns at a faster speed. She needed these training wheels to help her get to that place where she not only didn't need them but also found that they held her back.

When we are strong in our commitments to communicate and support each other's well-being, we feel strong in our relationships, even when we're moving into uncharted territory. We realize that traveling to places we haven't been before does not have to be a threat to our relationships because we know that we can be flexible enough to handle whatever happens.

Problems are a reality in all relationships. Whether we experience problems doesn't define the health of our relationship. How we deal with the problems that naturally arise and whether we have more than just problems in our relationships are better measures for the health of our relationships. If all we ever do is handle problems, our relationships are seriously out of balance becoming a place of drudgery.

Play

To keep our relationships healthy we need to create time for play. Playing together is absolutely essential for a healthy relationship. If we don't play, our relationships become solely about dealing with problems and handling all the details of life — what a drag! On the other hand, playing together transforms our relationships into a place where we have fun and enjoy ourselves.

When we feel honored, supported and loved by our partners, our desire to play and celebrate together grows. I feel truly blessed to share my life with three people in my family with whom I enjoy playing. I cannot tell you whether this is just luck or the result of our commitment to each other's well-being. We're too far gone to figure that out. All I know is that our commitments help keep our playfulness alive, which helps us get through our rough moments and then reconnect with each other when we finish forgetting and remember who we really are to each other.

Contrasting Commitment with Obligation and Duty

Commitment:	Obligation and Duty:
1. We have freedom of choice.	1. We have little choice.
2. We take responsibility ourselves.	2. We feel controlled by outside forces.
3. We focus on other's needs.	3. We focus on our needs.
4. We communicate.	4. We control.
5. Our mood is faith and trust.	5. Our mood is fear.
6. Problems don't threaten our relationships.	6. Problems threaten relationships.

Tool #12—Giving and Receiving Freely

When Ellen, a 28-year-old architect, came to see me, she said that she had been feeling depressed and having doubts about her relationship with her fiancé, Tom, a 32-year-old engineer. She described Tom as having a lot of great qualities that anyone would find desirable in a mate. He was loyal, dependable, caring, intelligent and attractive. But lately she'd begun to feel impatient and grown critical of him. She thought he was too concerned with money, even cheap. Last week, they had gone out to dinner with another couple. When the bill came, Tom began to figure out how they would split the bill to the penny, something he always did. Ellen got very upset, grabbed the bill and put the whole thing on her charge card. Afterwards, they had a huge fight that ended with her saying that she didn't know if she still wanted to marry him. Tom couldn't understand what the problem was; he was just trying to be fair.

Ellen described an earlier fight when Tom went with her to buy a birthday gift for a friend. Tom wanted to know what her friend had given Ellen on her birthday. When Ellen shared that her friend had only gotten her a card, Tom questioned why Ellen felt compelled to buy her a gift. Ellen replied that she just wanted to. Tom couldn't get it and wouldn't let the issue go, so they had another intense argument.

Whenever Tom acted too concerned with money, Ellen felt rage build inside her, and she just felt like screaming at him. She had thought about ending the relationship but, also feeling that they still loved and cared about each other, she didn't want to give up too easily.

Several sessions later, Ellen was 15 minutes late for her appointment. She'd been caught in a traffic jam because of an accident. I decided to extend our time together so that she could get a full session. The next session, she brought me a small gift as thanks for my generosity. When I asked her when she thought to get me a gift, she replied as soon as I told her I was extending the session. We spent the session talking about how her need to get me something in return might not be unrelated to the rage she feels about Tom's behavior.

Most of the things we do in our relationships are some form of exchange. Sometimes our exchange is spoken communication, and sometimes it is material in the form of some service or object. We can communicate how we feel, what happened today or our thoughts. We might do someone's laundry or give him or her a birthday present. In another mood, we might tell someone how angry we are with him or her or eat the last piece of birthday cake that they'd been saving for themselves. Whether positive or negative, these are all forms of exchange, and all exchanges require both giving and receiving. In some sense, giving and receiving is all that we ever do in our relationships.

The most important form of giving

Any form of giving will serve relationships; however, certain kinds of giving are essential to healthy relationships. Though material giving is necessary, relationships will suffer without a significant amount of personal communication. My wife appreciates the things that I give her, but my sharing of myself really strengthens our relationship. Material providing can sustain a relationship at a minimal level, but personal sharing makes our relationship grow and thrive.

To create and sustain healthy relationships we must share ourselves with each other. If I don't share my thoughts and feelings with my wife, our relationship will be undernourished and wither like a garden that doesn't receive enough water or nutrients. Sharing is the raw material for building healthy relationships. It's like the compost that can feed a struggling plant, turning it into a healthy, growing shrub with beautiful blooms that gives pleasure to everyone who sees it.

Learning to give freely

Giving nourishes our relationship only when we give freely. Giving freely means giving without concern for what we get back. When we give freely, we focus on what is best for the receiver of our gift. Our own interests are of little or no concern. Helping my daughter with her report without concern for whether I will get anything back from her is a true expression of my caring and love for her. My giving is a statement of how much I support her and how much I want her to succeed; it is an expression of my true feelings for her.

When we lack what we need to be happy and alive, we find it hard to give freely to others. Also, any unresolved feelings from not having our own needs met in the past will inhibit our ability to give freely to others. I can guess that Tom has some early experience of not having gotten his monetary needs met or at least someone making him think that there might not be enough money to go around. Maybe his parents were poor and there wasn't enough money to give Tom the present he wanted on his birthday. When we have unresolved, hurt feelings from not having gotten our needs met, any opportunity to give becomes a reminder and stimulus for feeling these bad feelings. Giving to others only reminds us of what hasn't been given to us.

Giving freely becomes easier when we resolve our hurt feelings from not having always gotten what we needed. This means identifying our feelings, owning them and, if necessary, expressing them. Then we can become free in our present giving. As we gradually resolve these feelings we gradually become freer in our giving to others.

Usually, seeing our needs left unmet made us feel hurt and unimportant. Also, if we identified with our experience, our sense of self worth suffered. As children, it's normal to feel that there's something lacking in us when we don't get what we need or want out of life.

In second grade, I didn't receive praise from my teacher for doing a good job with an assignment. Instead, I received a lecture telling me that it was wrong for me to have too much pride in myself. I immediately began, on a very deep level, to develop feelings of low self-worth, and I questioned my value as a human being. From then on, any good feelings that I had about doing something well were tempered with feeling that somehow I must be bad for feeling this way. Also, I began to find it hard to feel good when someone else received praise. Someone else's praise only reminded me of my own pain from not getting the praise I deserved.

We all have different experiences of not having gotten our needs met. Some of us might have feelings that we were undeserving because we didn't have enough to eat, while others of us feel bad because we didn't get enough attention. The origins of our bad feelings don't matter as much as knowing that we can uncover and resolve them.

Overcoming my jealousy of others required that I uncover and resolve my hurt from that time of not being praised as a child. Resolving my hurt feelings freed me to enjoy others' successes without the feeling that it meant something about me. Someone receiving praise didn't mean that I wouldn't when it became my turn.

In the same way, to be freely giving with his money, Tom needs to recover his memories that shaped his early learning about money. Identifying and resolving his feelings from these experiences will help him be more freely giving in the present without being concerned with what he gets back.

Working through our feelings

We work through our feelings by identifying, acknowledging and expressing them, and through healing our hurt. In the example above, my own healing began when a friend pointed out that I interrupted myself whenever I expressed feeling good about doing something well. When she confronted me, I realized that I had a problem. With her help I was able to recover some very painful memories associated with my feelings, and in turn these memories helped me get in touch with more of my feelings. Realizing that I had suffered a great emotional wound, I shared my feelings and memories with her and I began to heal.

When this second grade incident occurred, I not only learned to stop myself from feeling good about my accomplishments, but I also suppressed the part of me that feels excited and alive about new discoveries and accomplishments. I hid it behind a sense of guilt and shame that I was doing something wrong if I felt too good about my accomplishments.

As I released my hurt, I began to recover the energy and excitement that was so familiar to me as a little boy. Once again, it was okay to feel good about my accomplishments, as long as I remembered that my accomplishments didn't make me better than other people. By releasing my pain, I was able to better appreciate everyone's accomplishments. I freed up my ability to give because I no longer felt bad that I hadn't always gotten what I needed and wanted in my own life.

We can work through the hurt of any experience by becoming aware of what keeps us from being the truly generous people that we are at our core. When we get in touch with our hurt feelings and identify their source, we can release them and better distinguish between what happened to us and who we are. Bad things *can* happen to good people and sometimes for no real reason. Understanding how something came about, however, is not as important as freeing our sense of self from what happened. That something bad happened to us, or that we were treated poorly, doesn't make us bad. We also don't have to like what happened; we just have to accept it. Consequently, the more we accept our experiences, the more they empower us and the less they victimize us.

Giving freely is one of the purest forms of human loving. It is a truly selfless act in which we give to others from our heartfelt caring and compassion. In order to give freely we must truly get ourselves out of the way, and what we get out of the way is our sense of ourselves as being small, needy and unworthy. When we get out of the way, a sense of self emerges that is free, fully expressive and compassionate. Our attention is on what we are giving instead of what we can get back.

Receiving freely

In order for people to give freely, there must be people willing to receive freely, accepting a gift without immediately thinking about what they will give back. With my question in our third session, Ellen began to notice that she found it easier to give than to receive. She realized that she couldn't receive a gift from someone without immediately planning what she was going to give back. Though this seems like graciousness, it's not. By planning to give back immediately upon receiving something, she's not honoring the act of giving. Instead, she's acting out an old belief that it's not okay for her to get something without giving something back. Her need to give overwhelms the true graciousness of freely receiving something.

Feeling that it's not okay to get what we want also gets in the way of our giving freely. When we feel that it's not okay to get what we want, we can become addicted to giving. Giving becomes a drug that eases the pain of not having gotten what we deserved. People who are chronic givers suffer from a low sense of self. Their self-worth depends on being able to give because they have to give to feel good about themselves. This is not giving freely because they must give. Their giving is more a function of their own need to give than the needs of those they give to. Ellen's compulsion to give me a gift revealed her inability to freely receive a gift from me. When I asked her to imagine not giving something back to me, she experienced some excruciating pain that we traced back to deep hurt from feeling ignored and devalued as a child. Her need to give masked her pain that was rooted in her belief that she didn't deserve to receive gifts. We began to understand why she chose someone, Tom, who didn't give freely and why his stinginess also sent her into a rage.

Again, the solution lies in both resolving her feelings from not having gotten her needs met and transforming her sense of self. This will help her evolve from someone who feels she deserves to not get her needs met into someone who feels she deserves to get her needs met in spite of the reality that sometimes she won't. This wound that leads to not being able to receive freely requires serious attention. Everyone, including Ellen, deserves to feel valued for just being themselves, and everyone deserves the experience of others giving to them just because they are.

When we receive freely without needing to immediately determine what to give back, we give the gift that is the opportunity for someone to give freely to us. Giving freely is one of life's great pleasures; however, to give freely someone must be willing to receive freely. In a sense, then, receiving freely is really an act of giving. When we receive freely we give others the opportunity and pleasure of giving to us.

As a young man, I had an opportunity to learn a very valuable lesson about giving and receiving from my dad. When we would go out with other men his age I noticed that one or the other of them would pay the bill. One day, I asked my father why they didn't just split it. His reply was that when you split the bill every time you denied yourself two great pleasures, the pleasure of being treated and the pleasure of treating. This was a great lesson for me in the pleasure of giving and receiving.

I find it easier and much more pleasurable to give to my wife now that she's learning to receive my gifts freely. In the past when she would immediately go into her own giving mode whenever I gave her something, I felt that we were in some sort of competition around who could be more self sacrificing. My desire to give faded rapidly. I couldn't enjoy the good feeling that comes from giving something to someone just because I want to. Now, one of my wife's greatest contributions to my life is her providing a space within which I can give to her freely.

Being grateful

When others give to us, all that's required back is our thanks and appreciation. When we acknowledge someone's generosity we contribute to his or her sense of worth. Our thanks acknowledges their graciousness, and their confidence and trust that we live in a world where there is enough to go around. Because they believe that there's enough to go around, they can put their attention on giving without concern for whether there will be enough left to meet their own needs in the future.

Being grateful for the gifts we receive helps us create a world with a strong sense of connection and community. Our thanks honors the graciousness of the giver by saying that they can contribute to us in important ways that we appreciate. Feeling good about giving and grateful to receive, we experience a greater connection with each other. We create a reciprocity of giving and receiving based in our willingness to freely move from the gift of receiving to the gift of giving, and back again.

Greed and scarcity

The lack of free giving and receiving creates a world in which it seems that there's not enough to go around. It's a world where we find it difficult to give freely because we fear that we won't have our own needs met. Consequently, we base our giving on our desire to get something in return. It's also a world where we can't receive freely, fearing that no one would give anything to us if we don't give something in return. In this world we must take care of our own needs by either hoarding or bribing others to give to us by giving to them. We must take care of our own needs because we can't trust that others will take care of them. Therefore, we're constantly in competition for what seems like a limited amount of love, attention and caring.

The mood of this world view is greed. When we're greedy, we live in the misery of always being concerned with our own needs and competing with the needs of others. We live in a world that is lacking, where there's no possibility that everyone will get their needs met. We don't trust that our needs will be met, and we're always asking, "What's in it for me?"

Trust and contribution

Escaping this miserable world of scarcity requires trusting that we will be provided for because our needs are important and others want to freely give to us. When we truly trust and believe that others will provide for us, we can freely do those things that actually support getting what we need. When we ask "What can I contribute?", we will provide for others in ways that will help them feel valued and cared for. Subsequently, feeling valued and cared for, they become less concerned with their own needs and more able to provide for the needs of others.

Our challenge is trusting that if we focus on what we can contribute instead of what we can get, we will get what *we* need. This doesn't mean that we should never provide for our own needs or communicate that we need something. Often, we're the only ones that know exactly what we need, and sometimes we can best provide it for ourselves. I sometimes have a need to spend a few hours or a day by myself to recharge my batteries. Taking this time alone increases my ability to contribute to others. When I feel this need, I might have to turn down someone's request in order to take care of myself. However, taking care of myself is part of taking care of others. When we truly understand the nature of contribution, we know that we must take care of ourselves in order to be healthy and able to take care of others. We must be careful, however, that we don't get so preoccupied with getting our own needs met that we start to believe that there's not enough to go around. When we truly believe that there is enough to go around, we balance our needs with the needs of others, creating a natural flow in which our desire to contribute to the world includes ourselves.

If our attention is on what we lack, we never feel satisfied. Regardless of how much we have, we are always trying to get more and worrying about keeping what we have. We experience the frustration and misery of reaching for the elusive carrot at the end of the stick.

In contrast, when we focus our heart and attention on contribution, we feel satisfied with what we have. We can feel thankful for what we have instead of regretting what we lack, creating a flow of giving in which others feel more willing and able to provide for our needs. Thus, we end up living in a world of plenty where there's always enough to go around for everyone, including us. We give to each other freely and receive freely, creating a world of free and plentiful exchange.

Giving and Receiving

1. Sharing ourselves is the most important form of giving.

2. Giving freely means giving without concern for what we get back.

3. Receiving freely means accepting gifts without immediately thinking about what we will give back.

4. When others give to us we need only to be grateful.

5. Healthy relationships need both free giving and free receiving.

Tool #13—Integrating Dependence and Independence

Until now, I've discussed relationships as if they exist in a vacuum. However, all relationships exist in the environment of other relationships. My wife and I have relationships that we share as a couple, and each of us has relationships of our own. Our challenge is empowering our relationship to support our having healthy relationships outside our partnership and family.

In healthy relationships, dependence and independence are not opposites. They complement each other. In healthy relationships, dependence means being able to depend on others; it is not an unhealthy attachment where we rely on others to make us happy. In my relationship with my wife, I can depend on her for many things, including caring for our children, listening to me when I have something to say and supporting me in my profession. I can depend on her to keep her word and, when we have a problem, to do what it takes to work things out until we're both satisfied.

Dependence on my wife is a positive force in my life. It helps me feel safe and secure to know that no matter what happens out there in the world, I can depend on her to help me deal with it. She is there to listen and to help me process my feelings and figure things out. Knowing that I can depend on her allows me to go out into the greater community with more courage and a greater sense of security. I know that I can extend myself and, if things don't work out, I have a place where I can be sure that I will be cared for and nurtured. Being able to depend on my relationship allows me to be more independent in my life outside our relationship. This healthy dependence actually fosters my ability to be independent.

Unhealthy dependence

In an unhealthy dependency we rely on others to make us happy. We look to our relationships to provide for our needs, and we expect our partners to look to us exclusively to fulfill all their needs. We only feel safe when our partners always come to us to solve their problems and get their needs met. We perceive reliance on others as a threat to our relationships. If our partner goes to a friend to get some advice, we wonder why they didn't come to us, instead of being happy that they're taking care of themselves.

This kind of relationship is an unhealthy symbiosis where nobody experiences themselves as whole. We're just parts that need other parts to make us feel whole whether we're the helping person or the reliant one. We look to others to provide what's lacking in us, and we must provide what's lacking in them.

Even though this kind of unhealthy dependency is most obvious in marriages or other primary relationships, it can develop in any kind of relationship. We can become upset when our children go to other adults to get help, and we can become upset when our friends seek help from other friends.

Healthy dependence

In contrast, a healthy relationship with healthy dependence encourages us to do whatever will make us whole as individuals. We know that we'll be supported, even if this means going outside our relationships to get some of our needs met, because we feel invested in each other realizing our full potential as human beings. Consequently, the more we do to realize our full potential, the more whole we feel, and when we return we bring much more back to our relationships. When we feel whole, we feel more able and willing to contribute because our focus is not solely on what we need to get in order to become whole. When we feel whole, we can focus more on what we can bring to our relationships instead of what we get from them.

As I stated in the last chapter, occasionally I have the need to get away from everything to renew myself. Sometimes, I do this by spending some time in nature with a close friend. We go on these short retreats together where we help each other get spiritually replenished. I'm often able to get back in touch with my sense of who I truly am and recommit myself to what's important in my life. During these breaks from the routines of my life, I recover a broader perspective that empowers me to successfully deal with all the little stresses that can sometimes overwhelm me. When I come home from my retreat I'm a new man, one that my wife likes much better than the wreck that left. Because I'm more in touch with my commitment to her, having remembered how truly wonderful my family is, I'm able to be much more patient and attentive to them. In this way, my going outside our relationship to take care of myself serves my relationship through what I bring back.

In healthy relationships, we support our partners when they go outside the relationship to enrich their lives. Subsequently, they bring back the resources and learnings they've gained through their experience.

The difference between self-reliance and rugged individualism

Being in relationships where we rely only on ourselves for sustenance is like being on a desert island where we have to be entirely self-reliant. There's nothing wrong with self-reliance. However, when this reliance depends on isolating ourselves from others, our relationships fail to thrive from a lack of outside stimulation. Just as a young baby who receives no touching and communication fails to thrive, a relationship without outside stimulation will grow stagnant and die. When we isolate our relationships by limiting outside involvement, we fail to utilize all the resources that are available in the greater community.

We live in a culture that romanticizes self-reliance and rugged individualism. In the not too distant past, we had to rely on ourselves to provide most of the things that we needed for survival. When we wanted to eat we grew our own food. This is particularly true in our American culture where we were living in the wilderness only a couple of centuries ago. Even in Europe, before the industrial revolution and the development of mechanical transportation, most people had to be much more self-reliant then we are today.

The great American myth is that of the pioneer who goes into the wilderness and carves out a living from what is available there. That myth no longer applies. We live in a world where we rely on others to provide for our basic needs, and we all contribute to the needs of others. I don't grow all my food, nor do I make my own clothes. Increasingly, reliance on others to help us requires learning to live in community with other human beings, accepting our mutual dependence as an evolutionary step. We need to realize that getting help from others is not a sign of personal weakness.

We have falsely equated self-reliance with rugged individualism, failing to see that true self-reliance includes getting help from others. When we're truly self-reliant we know when to get help from others because getting help appropriately is an act of self-reliance. We live in a complex world where it's almost impossible for any one person to know how to do everything. To take advantage of all the available knowledge and resources we must learn to rely on others' help. When my daughter needed stitches for a bad cut on her scalp, I got help from medical professionals. When my car needed the timing belt changed, I let my mechanic handle it. This doesn't mean that we have to rely on others for everything, just that there's too much to know to be able to do everything. A little knowledge about something can help us decide where to go for help, but if we try to do everything ourselves, our time and capacity for knowing will be stretched thin.

Not getting help when we need it changes self reliance into an addiction to rugged individualism where we think getting help is a weakness. This addiction to rugged individualism is an artifact from the past that no longer serves us in today's world. It is left over from a time when our survival may actually have depended on our being totally self-reliant. However, we now live in a world where we need to be in community with others so that we can work together to better provide for each other.

Family isolation

In the same way that we have isolated ourselves through romanticizing rugged individualism, we sometimes isolate our families from the greater community. We think that any desire or need to go outside the family to get a need met is an indication that something is lacking in our families. Something is wrong if our families can't meet all our needs. We experience going outside the family as a threat to the survival of the family. This attitude has created a world of isolation where we feel cut off from others without any sense of community. This is a real problem in today's world where many of us live some distance from our extended families. We need to begin to create extended relationships in a community composed of friends and neighbors willing to support each other in creating and maintaining healthy families.

In our family, our school provides a sense of community for us. We send our girls to a Friends School that has a particular philosophy about community and service. When we go to school we engage other families with similar values. We join these people at school workdays, and we therefore feel close and committed to the school, the teachers, the students and their families.

Why we don't get help

Many of us resist getting help from others because we think relying on others is a sign of personal weakness. We experience any reliance on others as proof of our personal inadequacy. I frequently hear people say that they feel better if they can do it themselves. Particularly in relationships, we falsely believe that we should already know how to successfully relate to each other. So if we seek help for our relationships, there's something wrong with us. Nothing could be farther from the truth.

Relationships evolve. How we created successful relationships in the past is no longer sufficient for creating successful relationships now. Not getting help when we experience problems in our relationships is like thinking that we should be able to drive a car because we know how to ride a horse. Some of the skills of riding might apply to driving, but we need new learning. The skills that served us in creating healthy relationships in the past are now not enough to create and maintain healthy relationships now. We look to get more out of our relationships, so it makes sense for us to work together to create relationships that serve us better.

In my work, I have repeatedly heard people say that they feel bad when they've had to rely on others to get through tough times. They felt weak for needing help. This attitude comes from their fears that others might not be interested in their well-being. Consequently, they feel safer relying on themselves. Some of us can extend their trust to our family members and a few friends, but the basic attitude is that they are a lot better off if they do it themselves.

Trust is not blind

Trust is the issue. Do we trust that most people in most situations are basically good and considerate of others? Can we rely on others helping us when we need it, and do we trust that we'll survive our hurt when they don't?

Whether to trust people is a difficult dilemma. On the one hand, if we don't trust others, we isolate ourselves and must rely on ourselves and a few close people to meet all of our needs. On the other hand, if we do trust, we expose ourselves to the mistakes that others might make, whether through bad intention or innocent negligence, exposing ourselves to the risk of being hurt and disappointed.

The solution to this dilemma is recognizing that trust is not blind, that we can use our perceptions and judgment to make intelligent and thoughtful choices about trust. The issue is not whether we trust others, but really whether we trust our own ability to decide whom and when we can trust. The answer to this question separates human beings into two groups.

One group is composed of those who don't trust their ability to decide whom to trust. These people approach the world with a basic sense of distrust, using their perceptions and discriminating abilities to find those rare places where they can trust. This attitude and life strategy supports the belief that the world is basically unsafe with a few havens of safety. People who approach life this way spend their time and energy checking to find whether situations are safe and protecting those safe places they've already identified. This is the consciousness of the Cold War, where we had to build large stockpiles of weapons to protect us because we couldn't trust others to cooperate with us in this unsafe world.

In contrast, the other group is composed of those who basically believe that the world is a safe place, trusting their ability to use their intelligence and perception to detect those places that aren't safe. They trust that they can determine where it's unsafe to venture and avoid these places until they become safe. With this attitude, we use our ability to communicate to create larger areas of safety. We experience other people as our potential allies rather than our adversaries, and we believe that we can resolve most problems through communication.

Emotional safety

Though I've used some analogies such as the Cold War that are about physical safety, I'm really talking about emotional safety here. In relationships, it's usually emotional safety that's at stake. We don't extend ourselves because we fear being emotionally hurt. We fear that our partners will go out, meet other interesting people whom they like better than us and decide that they no longer want to be in relationship with us. Well, if our fear is that we will lose others, then the best way to guarantee losing them is to be controlling, possessive and jealous. Being controlling and possessive of others gives them the message that we don't trust them. We disempower others with our lack of trust and eventually they leave because who wants to be in an intimate relationship with someone who doesn't trust you?

The best way to make our relationships last is by trusting and supporting our partners in creating their richest and fullest experience of life. Because we're supportive, they'll associate any positive experiences they have with our support. When I support my daughter in creating relationships with her teachers that nurture her learning and growth, she feels good about our relationship. Consequently, she'll want to be more open with me in order to share her excitement about the good things that are happening at school. Our supportive attitude expands our relationships to include all the things we do outside our relationships. Through unqualified support we create relationships that have the flexibility to include all our extended relationships.

Emotional safety is different from physical safety and the rules that apply to physical safety don't apply to emotional safety. No one ever died from a hurt feeling or a broken heart. I don't mean to belittle the emotional pain of some experiences like rejection, only to point out that when we allow ourselves to move through our feelings, we get over them. The way past emotions is through them.

I had many relationships that didn't last before I met and subsequently married my wife. Actually, all of my relationships before my marriage ended. If I hadn't allowed myself to move through my feelings of hurt and grief, when I met my wife, I might not have been open enough to pursue a relationship with her. If my previous relationships hadn't ended, I wouldn't have been available to be in a relationship with my wife. One irony of relationships is that the ending of one relationship creates the space for another.

Learning to trust

We can learn to trust our ability to detect whether situations are safe or not by learning from our experience and through the experience of others. Every relationship is a building block for the next one when we insist that we learn from our experience. Sometimes it takes time to learn lessons, however, we can use every experience we have to help us evolve the ability to be good and loving partners. Experience can be the great teacher if we allow it to be.

Learning that we can survive the hurt of painful experiences gives us courage to move forward into intimacy. Each of us has survived every painful feeling that we've ever had. When we acknowledge this, avoiding pain becomes less important in our decisions. We courageously move forward, knowing that taking the risk of being hurt is the doorway to the joy of intimacy.

Many sitcoms spoof the scenario of someone not asking for what they want because they're afraid of rejection, only to find out too late that what they wanted was there for the asking. If avoiding pain plays too large a role in our decisions, then we will consistently fail to get the things we want. Giving some of our attention to avoiding pain is important in order to avoid or get out of abusive situations. However, in most circumstances an extreme or primary concern with avoiding emotional pain will keep us from ever getting the intimacy we really want.

When we expand our definition of self-reliance to include relying on others, trust our ability to determine when situations are not safe and realize that we can survive our painful emotions, we're ready to fully embrace life and recognize that we're all already in relationship. We can now be in community with all other human beings, joining together to create a world that we can feel proud to leave to our children. If we look closely, we may notice that many of the children being born and raised today are better able to be in relationship and community with each other. To join them in this world it's imperative that we adopt inclusive attitudes that freely allow us to feel safe in our close relationships and that will help us extend ourselves to include our greater community in the circle of our lives.

Integrating Dependence and Independence

1. Healthy dependence and independence support each other.

2. Healthy dependence means being able to depend on others.

3. In healthy relationships, we support our partners when they go outside the relationship to enrich their lives.

4. True self reliance includes getting help from others.

5. Trust means believing in our ability to determine when situations are safe.

6. Trusting, we experience other people as potential allies.

7. We can survive all painful emotions.

Tool #14—Ritual and Celebration

Our cat died two days ago. Bugs was 16 years old and had lived a good life. She didn't suffer, dying soon after she began to decline. Yesterday, my daughters helped me pick a spot back in the woods behind our house where I dug a hole for her body. Digging the hole helped me feel more connected to her dying. When we buried her, my wife and I told our girls the story of how we first got her. We told them about her brother who had died when they were just two years old, and how she got all her funny quirks and behaviors. A lot has happened in these 16 years and we talked about that some. When we finished, my daughters covered her grave with rocks so that the animals couldn't unearth her. Later, I called a friend of ours, who had established a connection with Bugs this past summer when she visited us, to tell her that Bugs had died. I cried a little that night.

Ritual is a difficult subject for me because I've always found it hard to invite ritual into my own life. My earliest memories of ritual are religious rituals when I was told what to do and how to do it. There seemed to be little relationship between these religious rituals and my everyday life. Occasionally, a sermon was inspiring, but I felt uncomfortable for the most part and alienated by what seemed to be hypocrisy. As a young teenager, I rejected my religious upbringing and, as so many others of my generation, declared myself an agnostic. I couldn't relate to the idea of a paternal, distant God filled with vengeance, and if this was the only vision of God available, then maybe there was no God. I adopted the religion of science, believing we could directly observe what was real and needed only to measure and study physical reality in order to discover what was true.

Fortunately, I discovered in my late teens that there was more to life, that there was some higher power and however you might wish to describe it, something more than physical reality existed. I studied many of the great religious traditions and discovered certain threads that seemed to weave through all of them. I came to believe that there is a spiritual reality that is the source of our physical being. In my studies, I felt put off by those religions that professed to be the right and only true religion. Instead, I came to believe that all religious paths have merit, with every individual having the right to choose their own path. Accepting that I was a spiritual human being, spiritual considerations became a central and important part of my life.

Even though I'd decided that I was a spiritual being, I still had problems with ritual. My early negative experiences still influenced me, and when others invited me to join in ritual, I would feel very uncomfortable and try to avoid it. Recently, however, I've concluded that ritual is an important part of life, providing a way to express and acknowledge our commitments and who we're willing to be for each other. I discovered that we can make ritual relevant so that it becomes a natural extension of everyday living.

Ritual in relationships

My first experience of a meaningful and relevant ritual was my marriage. While planning our marriage, my wife and I realized that we couldn't relate to the traditional vows, so we created a ceremony with vows that expressed what being married meant to us. We borrowed from many different sources, creating a ceremony that expressed what we wanted to share with our relatives and friends. I felt deeply moved by this experience and began to entertain the idea that ritual might be an important part of any relationship.

Ritual can do many things for a relationship. A ritual is a marking, a time when we get our bearings and take a reading of where we've been, where we are and where we're going. This accounting helps us get a sense of what is and isn't working in our relationships so that we can make thoughtful decisions about where we're heading. One of the rituals from my childhood was a perfect example of ritual serving this function, though by the time it got to me, it had become distorted, no longer serving its original purpose.

I was raised in the Jewish religion, and one of the most important holidays was Yom Kippur, what we translate as the Day of Atonement. This is a one day holiday at the end of the Jewish New Year's celebration, usually sometime in the early fall. As a child, atonement was presented to me as a time when we made an assessment of all we'd done in the previous year, admitted what we'd done wrong, and prayed to God to forgive us for our "sins." This ritual was rooted in the idea that all acts need to be judged as either good or bad and that we should feel guilty for our sins. My sins got a lot of attention. God was represented as omniscient, sitting in judgment of what we'd done, and if I didn't repent and ask for forgiveness, I was in deep trouble. This was a grim and scary holiday for a little kid.

I suspect that many in my religious community had a different sense of this holiday. However, because the scriptures we used were from a very distant time in the past, we've lost much of what I believe to be the original and true spirit of this holiday. We can find the true spirit of Yom Kippur in the name of the holiday. Yom Kippur is the Day of Atonement, at-one-ment. At-one-ment is the experience of our personal connection with God, a time to reconnect with our sense of who we truly are. It is a time to realize that at our core we are intimately connected to the Divine, and our only real sin is that we forget this. It is a time to recognize our false illusions of being separate from God, take responsibility for what we've done in the past year to separate ourselves from God and decide how we can change to connect more.

Rituals help us remember

So one reason for having ritual in our lives is to reconnect to our sense of who we truly are. We don't have to share the same beliefs or even be spiritual in any way to realize that there's something bigger in our lives than dealing with the day to day details of living. However, we do need to take the time to remember that we're a part of some larger community and confirm who we're committed to being for each other. This is one purpose of ritual, to ensure that we take time to step back from our lives and reconnect to the meaning that is important to us.

Taking time out is very important. Native Americans would frequently take time for rituals. They would have many rituals through the course of a year, and a ritual accompanied every important event. They marked and celebrated every significant change in a person's life with an appropriate rite of passage. Even individuals would take time alone to connect with their inner being through some form of retreat. They would go off alone into the woods on vision quests to fast and seek a vision that would reveal their true nature and purpose in this life.

Rituals are a time for remembering. When we engage in the normal activities of daily living, we can forget why we're doing all this in the first place. Rituals help us step back and take the space we need to remember our connection to each other. These ritual times allow us to remember our commitments. Reconnecting to our commitments, we regain the energy that originally accompanied these commitments, an energy that can erase the lethargy of living life disconnected from a sense of greater purpose.

Using rituals to create our future

In addition to being a time for measuring how our life has been going and reconnecting to our commitments, rituals are a time to create a vision for the future. They're times for us to consider what direction to take and how to get where we want to go.

Life is a series of phases in which what is appropriate for one phase of life is not necessarily appropriate for the next. The family with preschool children will do very different things than the family with grown children in college. The same commitment can take very different forms in these two families. Ritual is an opportunity to acknowledge our changes in circumstances and create ways to translate our commitments to fit the next phase in our lives. Using ritual to design a vision for our lives helps us become more conscious and intentional in our lives. Instead of sleepwalking through life, we consciously choose a path that we take willingly with our eyes open.

Nurturing and celebration

Ritual also serves as a time for nurturing each other. During rituals, we stop our normal activities. Many of the rules passed down to us in our religious traditions had the original intention of ensuring that we took a break from our everyday routines. When we forget all about work and get away from activities that isolate us from each other, we can better attend to each other. We can listen to each other without distraction and express our appreciation for each other. It can also be a time for giving to each other. When my wife and I were first living together, we would take time each week for one of us to give a massage to the other. This was a wonderful way for us to ensure that we would nurture each other on a regular basis. Though not formal, this regular massage was a ritual in our lives that helped us stay connected with each other.

Ritual is a time for celebration. It's a time for recognizing all that we've achieved in our lives together and acknowledging ourselves for our contribution to each other. Celebrating life is essential. Rituals help us celebrate the gift that is our being together. Celebrating our relationships helps us recognize the good aspects of our relationships and inspires us to live together in ways that beg celebration. This is the great spiral of life, where living and celebration begin to melt together and create the beauty that is life manifesting as love in the form of relationship.

Epilogue—Why Relationships?

We are in the midst of a dramatic evolution in consciousness. We're living into a time of greater and greater freedom, with responsibility replacing obligation and duty as the force that defines the boundaries of our living together. Responsibility requires a greater awareness, helping us know what our choices are and the ramifications of our choices. This greater awareness propels us into being more compassionate and understanding of each other so that we can make choices that will work for the good of all of us.

To make healthy choices we must clear away the old patterns that have imprisoned us in the illusion that we are separate from each other and that there is not enough to go around. Living in this illusion has allowed us to behave in ways that have damaged us and created a world where we're in competition with each other. It makes us focus on how we're different from each other, rather than how we're the same. We have created a world where we feel alienated from each other and afraid to be kind for fear of being hurt.

Each of us has a lot of work to do clearing away our old patterns that make us unkind and sometimes even cruel with each other. We must transcend these old patterns and false identifications, learning to act more consistently in ways that support the growth and well-being of those we love.

I believe that relationships serve as the playing field for this work. The challenge of creating healthy, alive relationships will spur us on to breakthroughs in our ability to be responsible and loving human beings. Our relationships are our field for learning how to be more fully who we are.

They are where we can allow ourselves to learn how to care for each other and treat each other with true loving kindness.

My hope is that reading this book will enable you to use your relationships as the arena for your growth and evolution as human beings. I hope that the distinctions I offer here will empower you to create relationships that are fulfilling and help you express the love you feel through your contribution to others. As we evolve together, we will naturally create stronger connections, creating a world that works better for all people. Our loving and caring is the cornerstone for a world that we can bequeath to our children, knowing that we left it in better shape than we found it.

Bless you.

Quick Order Form

Fax orders: 919-831-1103

Telephone orders: 919-755-0370

Have Your Credit Card Ready.

Email orders: orders@Hippo-Press.com

Postal orders: Hippo Press, P.O. Box 12948
                         Raleigh, NC 27605, U.S.A.

Quantity	Book Title	Per Item	SubTotal
	PARTNERSHIP TOOLS	$17.95	

Sales tax: Please add 6% for products shipped to North Carolina addresses.	**Tax**
Shipping by air: U.S.A. $4 for first book and $2 each additional book.	**Shipping**
	TOTAL

Method of Payment: ❑ Check   ❑ Credit Card

Kind of Card: ❑ Visa ❑ MasterCard ❑ AMEX

Card Number: _____

Name On Card: _____

Expiration Date: _____

Name_____

Address _____

City_____State_____Zip _____

Telephone _____

Email address _____

Please send more information on:

   ❑ Other books ❑ Speaking Seminars ❑ Consulting

Quick Order Form

Fax orders: 919-831-1103

Telephone orders: 919-755-0370
Have Your Credit Card Ready.

Email orders: orders@Hippo-Press.com

Postal orders: Hippo Press, P.O. Box 12948
Raleigh, NC 27605, U.S.A.

Quantity	Book Title	Per Item	SubTotal
	PARTNERSHIP TOOLS	$17.95	

Sales tax: Please add 6% for products shipped to North Carolina addresses.

Shipping by air: U.S.A. $4 for first book and $2 each additional book.

Tax	
Shipping	
TOTAL	

Method of Payment: ❑ Check   ❑ Credit Card

Kind of Card: ❑ Visa ❑ MasterCard ❑ AMEX

Card Number:_____

Name On Card: _____

Expiration Date: _____

Name_____

Address _____

City_____State_____Zip _____

Telephone _____

Email address _____

Please send more information on:
  ❑ Other books ❑ Speaking Seminars ❑ Consulting

Quick Order Form

Fax orders: 919-831-1103

Telephone orders: 919-755-0370
Have Your Credit Card Ready.

Email orders: orders@Hippo-Press.com

Postal orders: Hippo Press, P.O. Box 12948
Raleigh, NC 27605, U.S.A.

Quantity	Book Title	Per Item	SubTotal
	PARTNERSHIP TOOLS	$17.95	

Sales tax: Please add 6% for products shipped to North Carolina addresses.

Shipping by air: U.S.A. $4 for first book and $2 each additional book.

Tax	
Shipping	
TOTAL	

Method of Payment: ❑ Check   ❑ Credit Card

Kind of Card: ❑ Visa ❑ MasterCard ❑ AMEX

Card Number:_____

Name On Card: _____

Expiration Date: _____

Name_____

Address _____

City_____State_____Zip _____

Telephone _____

Email address _____

Please send more information on:
    ❑ Other books ❑ Speaking Seminars ❑ Consulting